FORT WORTH LIBRARY

W9-BXV-047

CHILDREN 970.00497 CONLEY
    2011
Conley, Robert J.
The Cherokee

Ridglea   08/18/2011

RIDGLEA BRANCH

The
Cherokee

THE HISTORY & CULTURE of NATIVE AMERICANS

The Apache

The Blackfeet

The Cherokee

The Cheyenne

The Choctaw

The Comanche

The Hopi

The Iroquois

The Lakota Sioux

The Mohawk

The Navajo

The Nez Perce

The Seminole

The Zuni

THE HISTORY & CULTURE of NATIVE AMERICANS

The
Cherokee

ROBERT J. CONLEY

Series Editor
PAUL C. ROSIER

CHELSEA HOUSE
An Infobase Learning Company

The Cherokee

Copyright ©2011 by Infobase Learning

All rights reserved. No part of this book may be reproduced or utilized in any form or by any means, electronic or mechanical, including photocopying, recording, or by any information storage or retrieval systems, without permission in writing from the publisher. For information contact:

Chelsea House
An imprint of Infobase Learning
132 West 31st Street
New York NY 10001

Library of Congress Cataloging-in-Publication Data
Conley, Robert J.
   The Cherokee / Robert J. Conley.
      p. cm. -- (The history and culture of Native Americans)
   Includes bibliographical references and index.
   ISBN 978-1-60413-796-5 (hardcover)
   1. Cherokee Indians--History--Juvenile literature. I. Title. II. Series.
   E99.C5C7158 2011
   975.004'97557--dc22   2010052647

Chelsea House books are available at special discounts when purchased in bulk quantities for businesses, associations, institutions, or sales promotions. Please call our Special Sales Department in New York at (212) 967-8800 or (800) 322-8755.'

You can find Chelsea House on the World Wide Web at
http://www.infobaselearning.com

Text design by Lina Farinella
Cover design by Alicia Post
Composition by Julie Adams
Cover printed by Yurchak Printing, Landisville, Pa.
Book printed and bound by Yurchak Printing, Landisville, Pa.
Date printed: June 2011
Printed in the United States of America

10 9 8 7 6 5 4 3 2 1
This book is printed on acid-free paper.

All links and Web addresses were checked and verified to be correct at the time of publication. Because of the dynamic nature of the Web, some addresses and links may have changed since publication and may no longer be valid.

Contents

Foreword by Paul C. Rosier   6

1   Introduction   14

2   The Coming of the White Man   26

3   Colonial Wars   33

4   Struggle Against Removal   38

5   The Trail of Tears   50

6   The Civil War and Indian Territory   59

7   The Three Tribes   68

8   The Cherokee Today   86

Chronology and Timeline   90
Glossary   96
Bibliography   100
Further Resources   102
Picture Credits   104
Index   105
About the Contributors   111

Foreword
by Paul C. Rosier

Native American words, phrases, and tribal names are embedded in the very geography of the United States—in the names of creeks, rivers, lakes, cities, and states, including Alabama, Connecticut, Iowa, Kansas, Illinois, Missouri, Oklahoma, and many others. Yet Native Americans remain the most misunderstood ethnic group in the United States. This is a result of limited coverage of Native American history in middle schools, high schools, and colleges; poor coverage of contemporary Native American issues in the news media; and stereotypes created by Hollywood movies, sporting events, and TV shows.

Two newspaper articles about American Indians caught my eye in recent months. Paired together, they provide us with a good introduction to the experiences of American Indians today: first, how they are stereotyped and turned into commodities; and second, how they see themselves being a part of the United States and of the wider world. (Note: I use the terms *Native Americans* and *American Indians* interchangeably; both terms are considered appropriate.)

In the first article, "Humorous Souvenirs to Some, Offensive Stereotypes to Others," written by Carol Berry in *Indian Country Today*, I read that tourist shops in Colorado were selling "souvenir" T-shirts portraying American Indians as drunks. "My Indian name is Runs with Beer," read one T-shirt offered in Denver. According to the article, the T-shirts are "the kind of stereotype-reinforcing products also seen in nearby Boulder, Estes Park, and likely other Colorado communities, whether as part of the tourism trade or as everyday merchandise." No other ethnic group in the United States is stereotyped in such a public fashion. In addition, Native people are used to sell a range of consumer goods, including the Jeep Cherokee, Red Man chewing tobacco, Land O'Lakes butter, and other items that either objectify or insult them, such as cigar store Indians. As importantly, non-Indians learn about American Indian history and culture through sports teams such as the Atlanta Braves, Cleveland Indians, Florida State Seminoles, or Washington Redskins, whose name many American Indians consider a racist insult; dictionaries define *redskin* as a "disparaging" or "offensive" term for American Indians. When fans in Atlanta do their "tomahawk chant" at Braves baseball games, they perform two inappropriate and related acts: One, they perpetuate a stereotype of American Indians as violent; and two, they tell a historical narrative that covers up the violent ways that Georgians treated the Cherokee during the Removal period of the 1830s.

The second article, written by Melissa Pinion-Whitt of the San Bernardino *Sun* addressed an important but unknown dimension of Native American societies that runs counter to the irresponsible and violent image created by products and sporting events. The article, "San Manuels Donate $1.7 M for Aid to Haiti," described a Native American community that had sent aid to Haiti after it was devastated in January 2010 by an earthquake that killed more than 200,000 people, injured hundreds of thousands more, and destroyed the Haitian capital. The San Manuel Band of Mission Indians in California donated $1.7 million to help relief efforts in Haiti; San Manuel children held fund-raisers to collect additional donations. For the San Manuel Indians it was nothing new; in 2007 they had donated $1 million to help Sudanese refugees in Darfur. San Manuel also contributed $700,000 to relief efforts following Hurricane Katrina and Hurricane Rita, and donated $1 million in 2007 for wildfire recovery in Southern California.

Such generosity is consistent with many American Indian nations' cultural practices, such as the "give-away," in which wealthy tribal members give to the needy, and the "potlatch," a winter gift-giving ceremony and feast tradition shared by tribes in the Pacific

Northwest. And it is consistent with historical accounts of American Indians' generosity. For example, in 1847 Cherokee and Choctaw, who had recently survived their forced march on a "Trail of Tears" from their homelands in the American South to present-day Oklahoma, sent aid to Irish families after reading of the potato famine, which created a similar forced migration of Irish. A Cherokee newspaper editorial, quoted in Christine Kinealy's *The Great Irish Famine: Impact, Ideology, and Rebellion*, explained that the Cherokee "will be richly repaid by the consciousness of having done a good act, by the moral effect it will produce abroad." During and after World War II, nine Pueblo communities in New Mexico offered to donate food to the hungry in Europe, after Pueblo army veterans told stories of suffering they had witnessed while serving in the United States armed forces overseas. Considering themselves a part of the wider world, Native people have reached beyond their borders, despite their own material poverty, to help create a peaceful world community.

American Indian nations have demonstrated such generosity within the United States, especially in recent years. After the terrorist attacks of September 11, 2001, the Lakota Sioux in South Dakota offered police officers and emergency medical personnel to New York City to help with relief efforts; Indian nations across the country sent millions of dollars to help the victims of the attacks. As an editorial in the *Native American Times* newspaper explained on September 12, 2001, "American Indians love this country like no other. . . . Today, we are all New Yorkers."

Indeed, Native Americans have sacrificed their lives in defending the United States from its enemies in order to maintain their right to be both American and Indian. As the volumes in this series tell us, Native Americans patriotically served as soldiers (including as "code talkers") during World War I and World War II, as well as during the Korean War, the Vietnam War, and, after 9/11, the wars in Afghanistan and Iraq. Native soldiers, men and women, do so today by the tens of thousands because they believe in America, an America that celebrates different cultures and peoples. Sgt. Leonard Gouge, a Muscogee Creek, explained it best in an article in *Cherokee News Path* in discussing his post-9/11 army service. He said he was willing to serve his country abroad because "by supporting the American way of life, I am preserving the Indian way of life."

This new Chelsea House series has two main goals. The first is to document the rich diversity of American Indian societies and the ways their cultural practices and traditions have evolved over time. The second goal is to provide the reader with coverage of the complex relationships that have developed between non-Indians and Indians over the past several hundred years. This history helps to explain why American Indians consider themselves both American and Indian and why they see preserving this identity as a strength of the American way of life, as evidence to the rest of the world that America is a champion of cultural diversity and religious freedom. By exploring Native Americans' cultural diversity and their contributions to the making of the United States, these volumes confront the stereotypes that paint all American Indians as the same and portray them as violent; as "drunks," as those Colorado T-shirts do; or as rich casino owners, as many news accounts do.

∗ ∗ ∗

Each of the 14 volumes in this series is written by a scholar who shares my conviction that young adult readers are both fascinated by Native American history and culture and have not been provided with sufficient material to properly understand the diverse nature of this complex history and culture. The authors themselves represent a varied group that includes university teachers and professional writers, men and women, and Native and non-Native. To tell these fascinating stories, this talented group of scholars has examined an incredible variety of sources, both the primary sources that historical actors have created and the secondary sources that historians and anthropologists have written to make sense of the past.

Although the 14 Indian nations (also called tribes and communities) selected for this series have different histories and cultures, they all share certain common experiences. In particular, they had to face an American empire that spread westward in the eighteenth and nineteenth centuries, causing great trauma and change for all Native people in the process. Because each volume documents American Indians' experiences dealing with powerful non-Indian institutions and ideas, I outline below the major periods and features of federal Indian policymaking in order to provide a frame of reference for complex processes of change with which American Indians had to contend. These periods—Assimilation, Indian New Deal, Termination, Red Power, and Self-determination—and specific acts of legislation that define them—in particular the General Allotment Act, the Indian Reorganization Act, and the Indian Self-determination and Education Assistance Act—will appear in all the volumes, especially in the latter chapters.

In 1851, the commissioner of the federal Bureau of Indian Affairs (BIA) outlined a three-part program for subduing American Indians militarily and assimilating them into the United States: concentration, domestication, and incorporation. In the first phase, the federal government waged war with the American Indian nations of the American West in order to "concentrate" them on reservations, away from expanding settlements of white Americans and immigrants. Some American Indian nations experienced terrible violence in resisting federal troops and state militia; others submitted peacefully and accepted life on a reservation. During this phase, roughly from the 1850s to the 1880s, the U.S. government signed hundreds of treaties with defeated American Indian nations. These treaties "reserved" to these American Indian nations specific territory as well as the use of natural resources. And they provided funding for the next phase of "domestication."

During the domestication phase, roughly the 1870s to the early 1900s, federal officials sought to remake American Indians in the mold of white Americans. Through the Civilization Program, which actually started with President Thomas Jefferson, federal officials sent religious missionaries, farm instructors, and teachers to the newly created reservations in an effort to "kill the Indian to save the man," to use a phrase of that time. The ultimate goal was to extinguish American Indian cultural traditions and turn American Indians into Christian yeoman farmers. The most important piece of legislation in this period was the General Allotment Act (or Dawes Act), which mandated that American Indian nations sell much of their territory to white farmers and use the proceeds to farm on what was left of their homelands. The program was a failure, for the most part, because white farmers got much of the best arable land in the process. Another important part of the domestication agenda was the federal boarding school program, which required all American Indian children to attend schools to further their rejection of Indian ways and the adoption of non-Indian ways. The goal of federal reformers, in sum, was to incorporate (or assimilate) American Indians into American society as individual citizens and not as groups with special traditions and religious practices.

During the 1930s some federal officials came to believe that American Indians deserved the right to practice their own religion and sustain their identity as Indians, arguing that such diversity made America stronger. During the Indian New Deal period of the 1930s, BIA commissioner John Collier devised the Indian Reorganization Act (IRA), which passed in 1934, to give American Indian nations more power, not less. Not all American Indians supported the IRA, but most did. They were eager to improve their reservations, which suffered from tremendous poverty that resulted in large measure from federal policies such as the General Allotment Act.

Some federal officials opposed the IRA, however, and pushed for the assimilation of American Indians in a movement called Termination. The two main goals of Termination advocates, during the 1950s and 1960s, were to end (terminate) the federal reservation system and American Indians' political sovereignty derived from treaties and to relocate American Indians from rural reservations to urban areas. These coercive federal assimilation policies in turn generated resistance from Native Americans, including young activists who helped to create the so-called Red Power era of the 1960s and 1970s, which coincided with the African-American civil rights movement. This resistance led to the federal government's rejection of Termination policies in 1970. And in 1975 the U.S. Congress passed the Indian Self-determination and Education Assistance Act, which made it the government's policy to support American Indians' right to determine the future of their communities. Congress then passed legislation to help American Indian nations to improve reservation life; these acts strengthened American Indians' religious freedom, political sovereignty, and economic opportunity.

All American Indians, especially those in the western United States, were affected in some way by the various federal policies described above. But it is important to highlight the fact that each American Indian community responded in different ways to these pressures for change, both the detribalization policies of assimilation and the retribalization policies of self-determination. There is no one group of "Indians." American Indians were and still are a very diverse group. Some embraced the assimilation programs of the federal government and rejected the old traditions; others refused to adopt non-Indian customs or did so selectively, on their own terms. Most American Indians, as I noted above, maintain a dual identity of American and Indian.

Today, there are more than 550 American Indian (and Alaska Natives) nations recognized by the federal government. They have a legal and political status similar to states, but they have special rights and privileges that are the result of congressional acts and the hundreds of treaties that still govern federal-Indian relations today. In July 2008, the total population of American Indians (and Alaska Natives) was 4.9 million, representing about 1.6 percent of the United States population. The state with the highest number of American Indians is California, followed by Oklahoma, home to the Cherokee (the largest American Indian nation in terms of population), and then Arizona, home to the Navajo (the second-largest American Indian nation). All told, roughly half of the American Indian population lives in urban areas; the other half lives on reservations and in other rural parts of the country. Like all their fellow American citizens, American Indians pay federal taxes, obey federal laws, and vote in federal, state, and local elections; they also participate in the democratic processes of their American Indian nations, electing judges, politicians, and other civic officials.

This series on the history and culture of Native Americans celebrates their diversity and differences as well as the ways they have strengthened the broader community of America. Ronnie Lupe, the chairman of the White Mountain Apache government in Arizona, once addressed questions from non-Indians as to "why Indians serve the United States with such distinction and honor?" Lupe, a Korean War veteran, answered those questions during the Gulf War of 1991–1992, in which Native American soldiers served to protect the independence of the Kuwaiti people. He explained in "Chairman's Corner" in the *Fort Apache Scout* that "our loyalty to the United States goes beyond our need to defend our home and reservation lands. . . . Only a few in this country really understand that the indigenous people are a national treasure. Our values have the potential of creating the social, environmental, and spiritual healing that could make this country truly great."

—Paul C. Rosier
Associate Professor of History
Villanova University

Introduction

The Cherokee have lived in the Appalachian Mountains for thousands of years. It has even been said that, when there are no more Cherokee in the mountains, there will be no more Cherokee. Their existence and their identity depend on their presence in the mountains. In fact, early mapmakers sometimes called the mountains the Cherokee Mountains. Cherokee towns were scattered over all or parts of what are now North and South Carolina, Kentucky, Virginia, West Virginia, Tennessee, Georgia, and Alabama. The Cherokee were a large and powerful tribe in the old Southeast. Many historians and anthropologists believe that they came to the Southeast from the Northeast, having been driven there by other Iroquoian tribes.

There are other stories as well. Perhaps the best-known story is one from the Cherokee oral tradition, recorded by James Mooney in the 1890s in Cherokee, North Carolina. It has the Cherokee originating in the mountains of North Carolina. In this story the earth is described as all water. It is covered over by a rock sky vault. The vault is like a giant bowl turned upside down, and all life-forms originally existed on top of the vault. According to the story, it became too crowded up there, and the animals decided to look for another place to live. Some of them came down from the sky vault, but they found only water. They decided to look underneath the water, and several different animals dived down, but they each came up with nothing.

The Cherokee were the largest and most powerful tribe in the Southeast. Residing mostly in the Appalachian Mountains, Cherokee oral tradition names North Carolina as the birthplace of their tribe.

Finally, a little water beetle said that he would try. The other animals laughed at him because he was so small, but he dived into the water anyway. He was gone a long time, but at last he came up carrying some mud he had found down there. The mud, though, was too soft to stand on, so after the beetle had spread it out on top of the water, the great buzzard flew over the mud, flapping his wings to dry it out. When his wings went down, they created valleys, and when they went back up, they sucked the mud behind them and created mountains. Then someone tied long cords to the four corners of this newly created earth and attached them to the sky vault. Someday, they say, the cords will break, the earth will sink, and that will be the end of the world.

THE WORLD

The world was seen as flat, floating on water underneath the huge sky vault. The sky vault tilted in the morning to allow the sun, a female, to come out and crawl along its underside. By nighttime, the sun reached the opposite side, and the sky vault tilted once more to allow it to go under and crawl along the top of the vault all night long.

There is another old story recorded by Mooney that tells of some Cherokee men who wanted to visit the top of the sky vault to see what was there. They traveled a great distance to the west, and at last they found the place where the sky vault came down to meet the earth. They waited for it to rotate, and when it began to rise, they tried to run underneath it, but it came back down before they could get to the other side, and they were crushed. No one else has attempted to make that journey since this disastrous first try.

CREATION STORIES

There are many stories from the Cherokee oral tradition that, when taken together, could be considered to be a creation, or origin, cycle, for they tell the way life here came to be. They are mostly animal stories, for in the oral tradition there is little, if any, difference between humans and animals. One story tells how the water spider captured the first fire. Lightning had struck a tree on an island in the middle of a river. The animals had been living in darkness and were cold. The lightning had started a fire deep down in the trunk of the tree, and the animals wanted the fire. Several of them tried to get it but with dire results. The blacksnake, known in Cherokee as the Climber, went to the top of the tree, but he fell into the fire when he went over the top and was burned black. The owl's eyes were filled with smoke when he looked into the tree.

Several other creatures were similarly marked, and they had just about given up when a little spider volunteered to try. The animals all laughed at her, but she decided to go anyway. She went across the top of the water to the island and entered the tree through a hole at the bottom. She saw a hot and glowing coal. Quickly she spun a small bowl and put it on her back. She put the coal in the bowl and returned to the other animals back across the top of the water.

Another story relates how animals and plants were obtained to eat. And there is one about how diseases came to be and how medicines to treat these diseases were obtained.

Then there are stories about Jisdu, or Rabbit, which are entertaining and educational. Rabbit is the Cherokee trickster. A trickster may do heroic tasks in one story and be cowardly or stingy in the next. He represents human beings in all their complexity. He shows us how we should or should not behave. Many of these trickster tales were borrowed and retold by African-American slaves. Joel Chandler Harris wrote some of them down as the Uncle Remus tales in seven books, beginning in 1881. "Br'er Rabbit and the Tar-Baby" is one of the better-known stories. They were retold again later in film in Disney's *Song of the South* (1946).

The oral tradition also contains monster stories and stories of warfare with other tribes. Taken together with songs and chants and charms, which are more like poetry, they form a formidable body of traditional Cherokee literature. Over the years Cherokee literature grew and developed, until today it includes many novels, poems, plays, and essays as well as the old stories from the oral tradition. Elias Boudinot, a Cherokee, wrote a short novel in the Cherokee language in 1833 titled *Poor Sarah, or The Indian Woman*. Few copies exist today. In 1854 Cherokee John Rollin Ridge wrote a novel, *The Life and Adventures of Joaquin Murieta*, which is still in print. Ridge also wrote a great deal of poetry and was named California's poet laureate.

Through the rest of the nineteenth century, there were many Cherokee poets and essayists, with most of their work appearing in newspapers. The early twentieth century, though, witnessed a great resurgence of Cherokee writing. John Milton Oskison wrote novels (*Black Jack Davy*, *Wild Harvest*, *Brothers Three*, *The Singing Bird*) and short stories ("The Problem of Old Harjo," "Only the Master Shall Praise"). He had two contemporaries who were equally successful: Rollie Lynn Riggs, whose play *Green Grow the Lilacs* was fashioned into the musical *Oklahoma* by Rodgers and Hammerstein and who also wrote *The Cherokee Night* and *Out of Dust*; and Will Rogers, who is best remembered as a humorist and an actor but who was also the highest-paid writer of his time, producing a widely popular newspaper column and several books. The tradition continues with novels, short stories, essays, and poems by Diane Glancy, Geary Hobson, Robert J. Conley, and others.

TSALAGI

The Cherokee speak an Iroquoian language, while most of the other southeastern tribes speak Muskogean languages (some Siouan and some Algonquian languages were also in the area). Culturally, the Cherokee shared many characteristics with the southeastern Muskogean tribes. Their songs and dances, their hunting-and-

Will Rogers

Known as Oklahoma's favorite son, the author, actor, and social commentator Will Rogers was one of the best-known celebrities in the United States in the 1920s and 1930s. Rogers was born into a prominent Cherokee family in 1879 in Indian Territory, near what is now Oologah, Oklahoma. His father was a Cherokee judge, and his mother was a hereditary member of the Paint Clan.

Young Will grew up on a ranch and learned how to rope cattle at an early age. Soon, his roping skills took him beyond the ranch, as he joined Texas Jack's Wild West Circus. In 1905, he made his vaudeville debut in New York City. The audiences enjoyed his rope tricks, but even more so, they loved the humorous monologues he delivered during his act. His commentary focused on intelligent and amusing observations about people, life, the country, and the government.

Rogers went on to become a Broadway star, and he acted in more than 70 films. In 1934, he was voted the most popular male actor in Hollywood. But he was more than just an entertainer. Rogers wrote 4,000 syndicated columns and 6 books and became a prominent political commentator.

In 1935, Rogers died in a plane crash in Alaska with his good friend, the aviator Wiley Post. He was 55.

Despite his stardom and fame, Rogers never lost touch with his roots. He and his wife, Betty, had four children and lived in California and on his ranch in Oklahoma. Rogers always enjoyed riding horseback and roping steers, and figured there was something wrong with anyone who didn't like a horse. Rogers was proud of his heritage and was billed during his career as "The Cherokee Kid" and the "Indian Cowboy." As he once said, "My ancestors didn't come over on the Mayflower—they met the boat."

gathering methods, their games, many of their religious ceremonies, and their reasons for and methods of warfare were all very similar.

The word *Cherokee* apparently comes from the Choctaw, and most often it is said to mean "Cave People." In the Cherokee language, they refer to themselves as *Tsalagi*. Before the use of that word became widespread, the Cherokee called themselves *Ani yunwi ya*, meaning the "Real People" or the "Principal People," or they called themselves *Ani Kituwagi*, meaning "People from Kituwah." Ani yunwi ya has come to mean "Indians."

Kituwah was an ancient Cherokee town, said to be the Mother Town of all Cherokee towns. In other words, all Cherokee towns grew out of Kituwah, which is variously spelled as Kituwah, Keetoowah, and Giduwah. Kituwah was lost to the Cherokee and for many years, white farmers worked the land where it stood. In 1996, under the leadership of Chief Joyce Dugan, the Eastern Band of Cherokee Indians purchased the site of old Kituwah, so it is once more in Cherokee hands. The Kituwah mound, once the foundation of the building that housed the sacred flame of the Cherokee, is still visible, although it has been worn down from years of plowing. The mound today is about 170 feet (52 meters) in diameter and 5 feet (1.5 meters) in height.

GOVERNMENT

The first we know of Cherokee history, the Cherokee were living in the Deep South. They lived in 80 or more towns and villages, and a typical town had about 200 to 250 residents. The Cherokee lived in three major areas known as the Upper Towns, the Middle Towns, and the Lower Towns. The people in each area spoke a different dialect of the Cherokee language. A story from the Cherokee oral tradition, printed in 1900 by James Mooney as part of *Myths of the Cherokee*, tells of a time when a powerful priesthood ruled the Cherokee. Eventually, though, the priests became too despotic, and a man whose wife had been taken by the priests while he was away hunting organized a revolution. He and his friends killed all the priests, and thereafter the Cherokee towns were democratic and autonomous, much like the old Greek city-states. According to the tale, the Cherokee never allowed a central government to develop among them again.

The old Cherokee government was democratic. A whole town would get together for a council. In any argument, the winning side was the one that kept talking the longest. In other words, when the opposition became tired of debating and quit, the winner was the side that had continued to talk.

Each Cherokee town had its own government, with a peace chief and a war chief. Each chief had his own councilors, representing all of the seven clans. The peace chief was in charge during times of peace, and he had control of all internal matters of government. In wartime, the war chief took over. He was probably also in control of all external matters of government such as negotiations with outsiders, including trade and other kinds of alliances. If a Cherokee town went to war, the war chief had no coercive power. He led by persuasion. If any of the men decided to quit and go home, they could.

Women were also very influential in government, but they did their part largely in the background, perhaps having recall power or final approval of any decisions made by the men. Some early Europeans complained that Cherokee men could not make up their minds. The Europeans would meet with the Cherokee, and at the end of the meeting, the Cherokee men would tell them to come back in four days and they would have an answer. At last, the Europeans found out that the Cherokee men were going home to talk with the women about the decision.

CLANS

The clan is all important in Cherokee life. There are seven Cherokee clans: *Ani-waya* (Wolf), *Ani-kawi* (Deer), *Ani-tsisquah* (Bird), *Ani-wodi* (Paint), *Ani-sahoni* (Blue), *Ani-gatagewi* (Wild Potato), and *Ani-gilohi* (Long Hairs). Most issues and problems

Will Rogers, a member of the Cherokee, was famous for his work as a humorist and an entertainer. In the early twentieth century, Rogers was a star on the vaudeville stage and transitioned into film.

that we today would consider matters for the police and the courts were settled by the clans. All Cherokee belonged to one of these seven clans, and every Cherokee therefore had relatives in every Cherokee town.

The Cherokee are a matrilineal people, meaning that an individual's descent is traced through the female line. Women had property and influence. A child is born into its mother's clan, and the father is almost irrelevant. A child's mother's brother is the most important man in the child's life, and a child has as many "mothers" as his or her mother and all of the mother's sisters combined. If a man was divorced from his wife, he had no alternative except to return home to his own clan.

GAMES

The Cherokee have always loved to play sports and to gamble. One game played long ago was called *gatayusti* in Cherokee, but it is more often called *chunkey* today. Chunkey is the Creek name for the same game. The game is said to have been invented by a man called Brass, who was passionate about playing it. In the game, players rolled a stone disk on the ground and tossed a spear after it. The object of the game was to have the spear touch the disk when the disk stopped rolling. It was scored by where on the spear it touched the disk or by how close to the disk the spear came. Spectators would bet lavish amounts on the outcome.

Another game that was played and bet on was *anetsa*, known in English as simply the ballplay, or sometimes, stickball. Large numbers of players were on each team. They met on a playing field similar to a football field with sticks in the ground at each end to mark the goals. Often one town would play another, or even one tribe would play another. The game was played with a ball roughly the size of a golf ball and with a pair of ballsticks about three feet long with a web at the end. The sticks were used to pick up, catch, and throw the ball. Anetsa was a metaphor for war. Sometimes tribes would settle disputes by actually fighting, sometimes by playing ball. There were instances when the Cherokee told white people that some Creek land, for instance, once belonged to the Cherokee, but "we lost it when we played ball against them." We don't know if they played a ball game or if they fought.

Another version of this game is played today in Oklahoma after an all-night stomp dance. In this version, there is only one goal. It is a carved, wooden fish on top of a long pole. The fish has a dowel-like piece coming out of its belly that is dropped into a hole in the top of the pole. The ball is thrown at the fish, and when the fish is hit, it spins. In this game men play against women. The men must use the ballsticks, but the women play with their hands. The women almost always win the game.

BALANCE AND HARMONY

In the old days, the Cherokee saw the world as made up of pairs of opposites: men and women, summer and winter, night and day, war and peace, and so on. Opposing forces were seen in the spiritual world, too. The early Cherokee described three worlds: the world on top of the sky vault, the world in which they lived, and the world below. Powerful spiritual beings lived in the world above and the world below. The world in between was seen to have been placed in a dangerous position. Therefore, maintaining a balance on this earth was all important. Many religious rituals and ceremonies had to do with maintaining the balance, or maintaining harmony. An annual cycle of seven major ceremonies was performed, with special ceremonies held when events called for them.

Some things were noticed that successfully crossed the boundaries between the opposites, and they were considered sacred. These included animals that stay up and hunt at night, like the owl and the panther; trees that do not lose their leaves in winter; or snakes that can crawl on the ground, climb trees, and swim in the water. All of these beings and others like them were considered very powerful.

THE POWER OF WOMEN

Cherokee men were primarily hunters and warriors. Women were farmers and homeowners, and in fact, they owned the farms and gardens as well as the houses. If a woman grew tired of her husband, she could throw his belongings out of the house and they were divorced. Women had a great deal of freedom and considerable power in old Cherokee society. In fact, the power of women puzzled early Europeans. One wrote, "A Cherokee woman will take a stick and beat her husband from his head to his heel, and when he can take it no more, he will turn over and let her beat the other side." He may have exaggerated some. Another said that the Cherokees had a "petticoat government."

The strength of the Cherokee women can be seen in the life of Nanyehi. In the mid-1700s, Nanyehi accompanied her husband to war against the Creek. When she was reloading his rifle for him, he was killed. So, Nanyehi picked up the weapon and continued the fight, killing several of the enemy herself. For that act, she was given the title War Woman. She later remarried and was known thereafter as Nancy Ward. It was during her lifetime, however, that women in Cherokee society began to lose their power and influence due to the incursion of white society.

The Coming of the
White Man

The first white people to visit Cherokee country were members of the infamous expedition led by Hernando de Soto. He and his men had come up through Florida, looking for gold and committing atrocities along the way, killing and enslaving hundreds or even thousands of Indians. The Cherokee had almost certainly heard of them and their barbarous ways before they saw them. From Florida, the de Soto expedition traveled through what are now Georgia, Alabama, Mississippi, Tennessee, Arkansas, and Oklahoma. They went through Cherokee country in 1540 and may have stopped at three Cherokee towns, but the Cherokee seem to have had a fairly easy time with them. The explorers went on their way, taking with them some dogs (or possibly opossums) that the Cherokee had given them for food. Still, while the Cherokee did not suffer at the hands of the Spaniards, they must have been aware that there were new

While searching for gold in the New World, Spanish explorer Hernando de Soto fought Chief Tuskaloosa and his followers in the Battle of Mabila in Alabama (*above*). Despite his pugnacious and destructive reputation, the Cherokee had a peaceful encounter with de Soto.

forces in the world, forces they would have to contend with in the future.

The Cherokee, however, did not meet Englishmen until 1673. They had not been bothered by white men for more than 100 years. But that year, two Englishmen, James Needham and Gabriel

Arthur, arrived at the Cherokee town of Chota in the Overhills on the Little Tennessee River. Needham and Arthur sought to open a trading path from Chota to the colony of Virginia. They were accompanied by a band of Occaneechi Indians, one or more of whom may have acted as interpreters, and a man called Indian John. Needham and Arthur were received well by the chief of Chota.

Needham left Arthur at Chota to learn the Cherokee language and returned to the colony for trade goods. He was accompanied by Indian John and some of the Occaneechi. On the way back, Needham and Indian John quarreled, and Indian John raised his hunting rifle and shot Needham in the head, killing him. Then he cut out his heart. He sent a message back to Chota to kill Arthur. The chief was away, and Arthur was tied to a stake to be burned. The chief returned before the fire was set, however, and demanded to know who was going to light the fire. A Weesock Indian who was visiting at Chota raised a fire brand and said, "That am I." The chief immediately shot the man dead and cut Arthur loose. Arthur lived at Chota for a year, dressing like a Cherokee and going on numerous raids with them, some against the Spaniards, some against other Indian tribes.

Arthur had kept a daybook while he was with the Cherokee, and from this daybook, we know that the Cherokee had guns in 1673. They may have obtained these guns from the Spaniards, either by raiding or perhaps by trade. Arthur's description of a Cherokee town was the first that we have. He described Chota as being built along a river with a 12-foot-high (3.7-meter-high) wall of logs surrounding three sides of the town. Scaffolds with parapets were used to defend the walls, and houses were built along streets in the town. Arthur was escorted safely back to Virginia by some Cherokee in 1674, and from that time on, many Englishmen visited the Cherokee, seeking trade or other types of alliances. During this time, the Cherokee are said to have made a treaty with South Carolina. If they did, the treaty has not survived.

Abraham Wood in a Letter, Based on a Description in Gabriel Arthur's Daybook

"The towne of Chote is seated on ye river side, having ye clifts on ye river side on ye one side being very high for its defence, the other three sides trees of two foot or over, pitched on end, twelve foot high, and on ye tops scaffolds placed with parapets placed to defend ye walls and offend theire enemies which men stand on to fight, many nations of Indians inhabit downe this river . . . which they the Cherokees are at warre with and to that end keepe one hundred and fifty canoes under the command of theire forts. Ye least of them will carry twenty men, and made sharpe at both ends like a wherry for swiftness, this forte is four square; 300: paces over and ye houses set in streets."

In 1711, officials in Charlestown (now Charleston), South Carolina, gave guns to the Cherokee in exchange for their agreement to fight the Tuscarora, with whom the colonists had already gotten into skirmishes. The Cherokee in league with the South Carolinians drove the Tuscarora out of the Southeast. The Tuscarora went to the Northeast, where they became the fifth tribe in the famous Iroquois Confederacy. Over the next few years, the Cherokee discovered that the colonists would deliberately start wars between different Indian tribes. They would give guns to both sides in exchange for all the prisoners that had been captured. The colonists then sold the prisoners into slavery in the West Indies. In 1715, the Cherokee joined with the Yamasee in fighting the South Carolinians. They made peace with the colonists the next year.

In 1721, 37 Cherokee chiefs met with Governor Francis Nicolson of South Carolina. They defined the boundary line between the Cherokee country and the South Carolina colony, with the Cherokee giving up land to the English colonists for the first time. Because the British were frustrated over having to deal with chiefs from different Cherokee towns, the Cherokee also agreed to appoint one chief to deal with South Carolina as a commissioner of trade. Upon returning home, they elected Wrosetasatow as commissioner of trade. The English selected Colonel George Chicken as their commissioner of trade.

In 1725, Great Britain sent Colonel Chicken into Cherokee country to regulate Cherokee-British trade and to get the Cherokee to side with the British against the French. Chicken said that the Cherokee's enemies were continually lurking about, within a mile of the towns. The towns were therefore fortified.

CUMING AND PRIBER

In 1730, Sir Alexander Cuming, an Englishman, showed up at Keowee, a Cherokee town near present-day Clemson, South Carolina, and met with 300 Cherokee. He got the Cherokee to swear allegiance to King George II of England, to promise to trade with no other country than England, and to name "Moytoy" as "Emperor of the Cherokees." (Moytoy is obviously Cuming's attempt at spelling a Cherokee name, possibly Ama Edohi or some other similar name. English attempts at spelling Cherokee names are usually horrendous.) It is probable that the Cherokee saw the new "emperor" as nothing more than the trade commissioner they had appointed before. The English, however, thought of him as the actual emperor of the Cherokee. When Cuming returned to England, he took with him seven Cherokee men. One of these seven would later become famous as Ada gal'kala (Attakullakulla) or the Little Carpenter.

King George received the Cherokee in his court. They signed Articles of Agreement with England, agreeing to be allies in war and to conduct trade exclusively with England. Cuming and the English turned the Cherokee against the French.

After Sir Alexander Cuming met a band of Cherokee in South Carolina, the group swore their allegiance to the king of England. Later, when Cuming returned to Europe, a contingent of Cherokee accompanied him to London (*above*).

Six years later, another white man came among the Cherokee, Christian Gottlieb Priber. He called himself a Jesuit priest and was said to be a Frenchman. Priber claimed to have received the title "His Majesty's Principal Secretary of State" directly from Moytoy. He set out, it is said, to make the Cherokee Nation over into a communal state, with free love and with children being raised by the state. This seems highly unlikely, if for no other reason than the Cherokee have always been very fond of their children. It is nearly impossible to believe that a lone white man in those days could get the Cherokee, especially the women, to listen to such outlandish talk. Possibly this story is a result of English propaganda. Priber, however, did make friends with Oconostota, an influential war chief, and won him and his followers over to the French. English colonists, who believed Priber was an agent of the French, captured him in Georgia. He was thrown into prison, where he later died. His influence, though, lasted with Oconostota and his followers for several years.

The events with Priber seem to have left the Cherokee divided in their alliances with the Europeans. While most still backed the English, Oconostota and some of his followers remained partial to the French. In 1738, a smallpox epidemic swept through the Cherokee towns, possibly killing over half the population. After more than 60 years of contact with the English, it was apparent that the ways of the Cherokee had changed—they now had guns and ammunition, and they had developed a hunting and trading economy.

Colonial Wars

In the 1750s, England and France were at war in Europe, and that battle extended to the New World. Both sides tried to draw their Indian allies into the war. In 1756, colonists from Virginia talked a group of Cherokee into going into Shawnee country to kill Shawnees, who were allies of the French. During their pursuit, the Cherokee's boats overturned in an icy river, and they lost all of their supplies. Frustrated, they headed back home. On their way back, they appropriated some stray horses and took food from smokehouses and storage cellars in Virginia. The Virginians, unaware that these Cherokee were allies, attacked them and killed 24 of them. In 1759, a group of Cherokee killed 24 Virginians in retaliation. A battalion of Highlanders and four companies of Royal Scots under the command of Colonel Archibald Montgomery invaded and burned the Cherokee Lower Towns, killing 60 Cherokee and taking 40 prisoners.

In the meantime, Cherokee under Oconostota had surrounded the English Fort Loudoun and were trying to starve the
men in the fort into submission. Some Cherokee women who had
English husbands or sweethearts in the fort were smuggling food
in to them. Oconostota chastised the women, but they responded
by telling him that it was their duty to feed the men and that if any
harm came to them for their actions, their relatives would exact
revenge. Eventually, however, the siege worked, and the fort was
surrendered. The English agreed to leave the arms and ammunition in the fort for the Cherokee, and the Cherokee agreed to let
the English carry enough ammunition with them to hunt along
the way back. After the English abandoned the fort, however,
the Cherokee found that the English had dumped the guns and
ammunition into the river.

Angered by this deception, the Cherokee attacked the soldiers along the trail and wiped them out, except for taking a few
captives. One captive was John Stuart, who would later become
important in Cherokee affairs. He was nicknamed Bushyhead by
the Cherokee because of his head of wild red hair. When Stuart
was captured, his friend Ada gal'kala bargained with his captor
and saved his life.

The Cherokee sued for peace then, but the English, embar-
rassed by the surrender of Fort Loudoun, refused. Instead, they sent
Colonel James Grant with 2,000 men to invade Cherokee country.
Grant destroyed 15 Cherokee towns and 1,500 acres of corn, beans,
and peas, sending 5,000 Cherokee into the hills homeless and starving. When 24 Cherokee were killed, the Cherokee were satisfied by
killing 24 whites, but for those 24 whites, the white men sent more
than 5,000 Cherokee into the mountains to starve.

In 1761, the Cherokee signed separate peace treaties with
South Carolina and with Virginia. Lieutenant Henry Timberlake
agreed to go into Cherokee country as a sign of goodwill. He
lived with the Cherokee for six months, gathering material for his
Memoirs.

MORE CHEROKEE VISIT ENGLAND

When Timberlake was ready to return to Williamsburg in 1762, Ostenaco and two other Cherokee accompanied him. Along the way, Ostenaco declared that he wanted to go to England to see the king. Timberlake agreed and arranged the trip. This second trip was not nearly as successful as the first one. American Indians had visited England many times since then. They were beginning to seem commonplace. Ostenaco had to wait three weeks to get an audience with the king. Ostenaco and the other Cherokee drank much while in England and were often displayed in public. Timberlake sent them home but did not go with them.

During this period, many white traders and Cherokee women married, resulting in a number of families of mixed blood. Some of the family names were Pearis (later changed to Paris and then to Parris), Dougherty, Adair, and Bushyhead (from Stuart). The white men made their influence felt, insisting on being the heads of their households and on passing their surnames onto their children. It was the beginning of the undermining of the Cherokee clan system and the influential role of women.

"TREATY" OF SYCAMORE SHOALS

In 1775, a large number of Cherokee gathered at Sycamore Shoals in Tennessee to negotiate a treaty with the Transylvania Land Company, under the leadership of Richard Henderson and Nathaniel Hart. Daniel Boone was a silent partner in the Transylvania Company. The land that the company wanted to purchase included most of what are now Kentucky and middle Tennessee. The negotiation was illegal, however, because of a king's proclamation and the agreement signed in England by Ada gal'kala and others. Both of these documents forbade the selling of Indian land to anyone except the king of England. But Ada gal'kala and Oconostota, both old men by this time, wanted the treaty. They wanted guns to fight the Chickasaw. So they sold the land to Hart and Henderson. Dragging Canoe (Tsiyu Gansini), a son of Ada gal'kala, came forward during this gathering to formally protest the sale. Richard Pearis, a trader, joined him in the protest.

The old men, however, won the argument, and the treaty was signed. According to *The Cherokee Nation: A History*, Dragging Canoe said to Hart and Henderson, "You have bought a fair land, but you will find its settlement dark and bloody." Later, Dragging Canoe told Henry Stuart, the brother of John "Bushyhead" Stuart, about the "Treaty" of Sycamore Shoals:

> I had nothing to do with making that bargin [sic]; it was made
> by some of the old men, who are too old to hunt or fight. As for
> me, I have a great many of my young warriors around me, and
> they mean to have their lands.

John Stuart had become the British superintendant of Southern Indian Affairs by this time, and he took Dragging Canoe's side in the dispute over Sycamore Shoals. Bushyhead, though, was sick in bed. He sent letters to the illegal settlers on Cherokee land advising them to move.

Dragging Canoe, having sent his own warnings to these settlers, was ready to attack them, but Stuart, Ada gal'kala, and Dragging Canoe's cousin, Nancy Ward, who was a *ghigau*, or "Beloved Woman," all opposed going to war. Around this time, the American Revolution had also broken out. Dragging Canoe waited as long as he could stand it, and then he made plans to attack the settlements. Nancy Ward, however, sent warnings to the settlements. The whites were ready and waiting, and Dragging Canoe's attacks in 1776 were unsuccessful. One of his brothers was killed, and he, himself, was shot through the hips.

Early historians have characterized Dragging Canoe as a vengeful, white-hating full-blood and his cousin Nancy Ward as a "good Indian" and a friend of the white man. Later historians have viewed Dragging Canoe as a Cherokee patriot and Nancy Ward as a traitor. The truth is probably somewhere in between. As a Beloved Woman, Ward should certainly have been listened to. Dragging Canoe ignored her advice and counsel. While it is difficult to disagree with Dragging Canoe's attempt to protect Cherokee land, it is also difficult to fault Ward's attempt to retain the old Cherokee traditions of women's powers.

The Cherokee Nation and the Americans declared Dragging Canoe and his followers, who sided with the British loyalists, to be secessionists and outlaws. They kept fighting, though, and the colonists retaliated, destroying Cherokee towns and crops. When their towns were destroyed, Dragging Canoe and his followers moved to an area near Chickamauga Creek in Tennessee. They rebuilt there and became known as the Chickamaugans. Even though the Cherokee Nation had outlawed the Chickamaugans, the colonists retaliated against the main body of Cherokee and demanded land cessions from them for the actions of Dragging Canoe.

The Chickamaugans were assisted in their fight with the new Americans by the British, who provided them with food and ammunition. In 1780, Dragging Canoe and the Chickamaugans helped the British retake Augusta, Georgia, from the rebels. The next year they attacked American settlements near Nashville, Tennessee. When the Revolutionary War ended, though, in 1782, British support was gone. Dragging Canoe and the Chickamaugans continued their fight alone. They were promised support from Spain.

Over the next several years, the Chickamaugans continued to struggle against the encroachment into their territory by white settlers. Treaties were signed, but settlers still moved onto Cherokee lands. Raids, skirmishes, and frontier battles marked this period. In 1792 Dragging Canoe, the last of the great Cherokee war chiefs, died, and the leadership of the Chickamaugans was passed on to John Watts, Bloody Fellow, Doublehead, and Bob Benge. In 1794, Major James Orr led an invading force that once again destroyed the Chickamaugan towns. Spain had withdrawn its support of the Chickamaugans because of its war against Napoleon, and the Chickamaugans finally signed a treaty at Tellico Blockhouse. The wars were over.

Struggle Against
Removal

The Cherokee Nation changed drastically in the years following 1794. After the signing of the treaty by the Chickamaugans, a group of Chickamaugans led by Chief Bowl (or Bowles, or John Bowl) was on its way home to Alabama when it met a riverboat or a raft of white people with African-American slaves. The white men wanted to trade after learning that the Cherokee had some money. They sold whiskey, beads, and mirrors to the Cherokee. The next morning the Cherokee thought over what they had done. They told the white men that they did not mind paying for the whiskey they had drunk but that they wanted to return the trinkets and get back the money they had paid for them. The white men killed two of the Cherokee. Then Bowl and the rest of his men killed all the white men. They did not harm the white women or the slaves, but let them go on their way to New Orleans. Then, out of fear that both whites and the other Cherokee would be angry with them for breaking the treaty they had just signed, they did not go home. Instead they went on to Missouri, where they built new homes.

By 1800, the land holdings of the Cherokee had been reduced to about 43,000 square miles (111,000 square kilometers)—mostly in Tennessee, with some land in Georgia and Alabama and a little in North Carolina. In the meantime, Christian missionaries were allowed into the Cherokee Nation to teach and preach. Schools and churches were established. The government was now reorganized

Conversation Between President Madison and Col. John Lowrey, in Ross Papers, Thomas Gilcrease Institute of American History and Art

In February and March 1816, a delegation of Cherokee went to Washington, D.C., to request compensation for damages done by white soldiers traveling through the Cherokee Nation at the end of the Creek War. The following exchange took place between Colonel John Lowrey and President James Madison:

Colonel Lowrey: Father I now have the pleasure to be in your presence. I am directed by my National Council to take you, our Father, by the hand. This day was appointed by the Great Spirit for us to see one another. It makes my heart as glad to enter your house as it does when I enter my own house.

James Madison: I was apprised of your coming before you arrived at this place. It always gives me great pleasure to receive my friends in my house especially my red Brethren the Cherokees who have fought by the side of their White Brethren and spilt their blood together.

with written laws. A national police force called the Lighthorse was established. But all was not peaceful for the Cherokee.

Presidents John Adams and Thomas Jefferson followed the practice of forcing trade goods on the Cherokee and keeping them in debt so that they could bargain with them later for land cessions to settle the debt. From 1791 to 1819, the Cherokee signed 25 land cession treaties with the United States. In addition, Jefferson signed an agreement with the state of Georgia in 1802, known as the Georgia Compact, agreeing in exchange for Georgia's western lands to remove the Cherokee from within the state's boundaries as soon as could be reasonably accomplished.

In late 1811 and early 1812, those Chickamaugans who had removed themselves to Missouri suffered through a series of intense earthquakes that centered on the town of New Madrid. The quakes, which lasted from December 1811 to February 1812, were felt over an area of 50,000 square miles (130,000 square kilometers). Fearing to stay in Missouri, the Chickamaugans moved themselves into Arkansas. There they became known as the Western Cherokee Nation or, later, as the Old Settlers.

In 1820, the Reverend Cephas Washburn established a mission, called the Dwight Mission, among the Western Cherokee. When Washburn interviewed some of the Western Cherokee, like Degadoga, Blackfox, Dick Justice, and Blanket, he told them some Bible stories. The Western Cherokee maintained that the stories must have been borrowed or stolen from old Cherokee stories, for they were so similar. It seems likely that the Jesuit priest, Christian Gottlieb Priber, had told these tales to Cherokee back in the 1700s,

---

(Opposite page) When Europeans first arrived in North America, the Cherokee had more than 60 villages spread from present-day Alabama in the south to present-day Ohio in the north. By 1819, encroachment of American settlers whittled the Cherokee homeland to a fraction of its size. In 1835 they were forcefully evicted from it altogether.

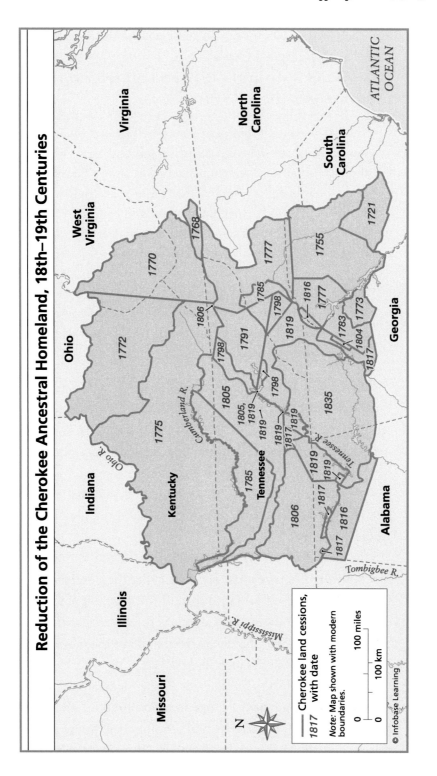

Reduction of the Cherokee Ancestral Homeland, 18th–19th Centuries

Cherokee land cessions, with date

1817

Note: Map shown with modern boundaries.

0 — 100 miles
0 — 100 km

© Infobase Learning

ATLANTIC OCEAN

Virginia
West Virginia
North Carolina
South Carolina
Ohio
Georgia
Indiana
Kentucky
Tennessee
Alabama
Illinois
Missouri

Ohio R.
Cumberland R.
Tennessee R.
Mississippi R.
Tombigbee R.

1721
1755
1768
1770
1772
1773
1775
1777
1777
1777
1783
1785
1785
1791
1798
1798
1798
1804
1805
1805, 1819
1806
1806
1816
1816
1817
1817
1817
1817
1819
1819
1819
1819
1835

and the Western Cherokee still remembered the stories but had forgotten their original source.

One example was told by Ta-ka-e-tuh to Cephas Washburn, as related in *Reminiscences of the Indians*:

> The first human pair were placed in a most beautiful country . . . disease and death were unknown . . . days and nights were of the same length . . . the temperature was always the same—never too cold nor too hot. . . . Then the animals could understand each other's language; and man could converse with all beasts and birds and fishes. . . . The first woman was walking by herself [when] the serpent addressed her in a very friendly voice . . . and induced her to violate the law of God. He then induced her to tempt her husband; and it was the serpent that gave her the power to prevail over the man and cause him to transgress. . . . It was eating the fruit of a tree, which the Creator had forbidden.

Back in the Southeast, the United States went to war with the Red Stick Creek in 1813, and 700 Cherokee joined with the U.S. Army in the fight. Many of these Cherokee would become prominent later. Among them were John Ross, Major Ridge, John Lowrey, Sequoyah, John Drew, White Path, Going Snake, and Junaluska. At the decisive Battle of Horseshoe Bend, it is said that Junaluska, known by a different name at that time, saved the life of General Andrew Jackson.

In 1817, Jackson, as a representative of the United States, met with the Cherokee and suggested that they exchange all of their land in the East for lands west of the Mississippi River. The Cherokee ceded some land in Georgia and Tennessee to the United States. Another 3,500 Cherokee agreed to make the move and join the Western Cherokee Nation in Arkansas.

Then, in an effort to forestall any further demands for land, the Cherokee Nation adopted a program of "civilization," encouraging mission schools in the Nation, and sending their young people to colleges and universities in the Northeast. Cherokee women learned

After 10 years of work, Sequoyah created an alphabet for the Cherokee language. It is the only known instance in history of an individual creating an entirely new writing system.

to cook, spin, weave, sew, mold candles, and sip tea. For any group of people to remake themselves, so well and so quickly, is a remarkable occurrence.

In 1821, Sequoyah presented the Cherokee with a syllabary, a system for writing the Cherokee language. It has been said that the Cherokee became literate in their own language almost overnight.

A national newspaper was established, called the *Cherokee Phoenix*. Its first editor was Elias Boudinot. Boudinot named the paper after the mythological Phoenix, the firebird that lives for 500 years, burns itself to ashes, and then rises from its ashes to live for another 500 years. He thought it was a good metaphor for the Cherokee Nation. Boudinot also embarked on a series of lectures in 1826 in New York and Philadelphia to bring attention to the Cherokees' fight to hold onto their ancient homeland and to raise funds for the newspaper and for an academy. The following poem honored Sequoyah's achievement:

ODE TO SEQUOYAH
By Alex Posey, Creek Indian poet

The names of Watie and Boudinot—
The valiant warrior and gifted sage—
And other Cherokees, may be forgot,
But thy name shall descend to every age;
The mysteries surrounding Cadmus' name
Cannot obscure thy claim to fame.

The people's language cannot perish—nay,
When from the face of this great continent
Inevitable doom hath swept away
The last memorial—the last fragment
Of tribes—some scholar learned shall pore
Upon thy letters, seeking lore.

Some bard shall lift a voice in praise of thee,
In moving numbers tell the world how men
Scoffed thee, hissed thee, charged with lunacy!
And who could not give 'nough honor when
At length, in spite of jeers, of want and need,
They genius shaped a dream into a deed.

By cloud-capped summits in the boundless west,
Or mighty river rolling to the sea,
Where'er thy footsteps led thee on that quest,
Unknown, rest thee, illustrious Cherokee.

CHEROKEE PROGRESS

As part of its effort at "civilization," the Cherokee Nation reorganized its government between 1817 and 1827. The government, like that of the United States, was a tripartite system. The principal chief was the head of state or the executive, a bicameral legislature was the legislative branch, and a judicial tribunal formed the judicial branch. The chief and the legislators were elected. The Nation was divided into eight judicial districts, each with a judge and a marshal. Taxes were levied. A national capital was established at New Echota in northwestern Georgia. The Cherokee wrote and adopted a new constitution in 1827 and appointed William Hicks as their first chief. In 1828, John Ross was elected principal chief of the Cherokee Nation, and one month later Andrew Jackson was elected president of the United States.

Despite the progress made by the Cherokee, the state of Georgia intensified its efforts to drive them out. Georgians and other southerners continued to press the president to remove the Indians from within their boundaries and live up to the 1802 compact. The Georgia Legislature passed a series of bills known as the anti-Cherokee laws in 1829. The laws prohibited the meeting of the Cherokee National Council, confiscated a large section of Cherokee land, nullified Cherokee laws within the boundaries of Georgia, provided for the arrest and imprisonment of Cherokee who influenced other Cherokee to resist removal, made it illegal for an Indian to testify against a white man in Georgia courts, and forbade Cherokee to dig for gold in Georgia on Cherokee land. The state of Georgia and the president were clearly in league with one another, and their aim was to make life so uncomfortable for the Cherokee that they would gladly move.

Sequoyah
and the Cherokee Syllabary

Sequoyah, who gave the Cherokee a system of writing and reading, was born in the mid- to late 1700s in Taskagi, in what is now Tennessee. His mother was Wuh-teh, the daughter of a Cherokee chief, and his father was Nathaniel Gist, a Virginia fur trader. The date of his birth is unknown, though scholars place it anywhere from 1760 to 1780.

Although Sequoyah was exposed to the concept of writing early in life, he didn't learn the English alphabet. A silversmith by trade, Sequoyah joined with other Cherokee in 1813 in fighting with General Andrew Jackson against the Red Stick Creeks. Around this time, Sequoyah began to think about the idea of literacy for the Cherokee people. Unlike white soldiers, he and the other Cherokee fighting with Jackson were unable to write letters home, read military orders, or record events. After the war, he began in earnest to create a writing system.

At first, Sequoyah tried to establish a character for each word in the Cherokee language. He did not succeed at his efforts, however, until he gave up trying to represent each word and instead developed a symbol for each syllable. With the exceptions of symbols for each of the six Cherokee vowel sounds and the sound for the letter "s," each symbol in Sequoyah's

In 1830, Jackson succeeded in pushing his Indian Removal Act through the U.S. Congress. Though it barely passed, the act called for the total removal of approximately 60,000 Indians from eastern lands to places west of the Mississippi River, whether or not the Indians agreed to the removal.

The Cherokee Nation, in response to Georgia's anti-Cherokee laws, hired famed attorney William Wirt, who took a case called syllabary stands for a complete syllable. For example, *Tsalagi*, the Cherokee word for "Cherokee" is written in the syllabary with three symbols rather than seven letters—*Tsa la gi*. Altogether, the syllabary consists of 85 symbols.

In 1821, Sequoyah presented his syllabary at Dwight Mission in Arkansas. Having convinced the Western Cherokee of its usefulness, he taught many of them to write in the Cherokee language. Sequoyah then had the people in Arkansas write letters to family and friends in the Southeast. He delivered the letters and presented the syllabary to the Cherokee National Council in the Southeast. The syllabary was accepted almost immediately, and most Cherokee became literate in their language in a brief time. Missionaries went to work publishing hymn books, translations of the Bible, and other religious tracts in the Cherokee language.

After the introduction of the syllabary, Sequoyah became a celebrity. He traveled to Washington, where he was feted, and the Cherokee Nation presented him with a medal. He continued to serve as a statesmen and diplomat in the Cherokee community. Sequoyah died in the 1840s during a trip to Mexico.

Whether Sequoyah actually invented the syllabary remains a question. Some believe that it was an ancient system that had fallen out of use and that Sequoyah had managed to salvage it and make it available to the people.

Cherokee Nation v. Georgia to the United States Supreme Court. Wirt argued that the Cherokee Nation was an independent, sovereign nation and therefore was not subject to Georgia's laws. On March 5, 1831, Supreme Court Chief Justice John Marshall declared that "an Indian tribe is not a foreign state . . . and cannot maintain an action in the courts of the United States . . ." and denied the motion for an injunction against the anti-Cherokee laws.

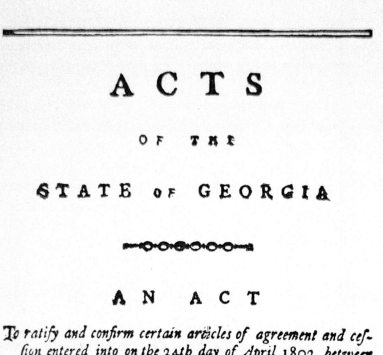

ACTS

OF THE

STATE OF GEORGIA

AN ACT

To ratify and confirm certain articles of agreement and cession entered into on the 24th day of April 1802, between the Commissioners of the State of Georgia on the one part, and the Commissioners of the United States on the other part.

WHEREAS the Commissioners of the State of Georgia, to wit: James Jackson, Abraham Baldwin, and John Milledge, duly authorized and appointed by, and on the part and behalf of the said State of Georgia; and the Commissioners of the United States, James Madison, Albert Gallatin, and Levi Lincoln, duly authorized and appointed by, and on the part and behalf of the said United States, to make an amicable settlement of limits, between the two Sovereignties, after a due examination of their respective powers, did, on the 24th day of April last, enter into a deed of articles, and mutual cession, in the words following, to wit:

ARTICLES of agreement and cession, entered into on the twenty-fourth day of April, one thousand eight hundred and two, between the Commissioners appointed on the part of the United States, by virtue of an act entitled, " An act for an amicable settlement of limits

The Georgia Guard then arrested 11 missionaries who had been living and working in the Cherokee Nation for their refusal to sign an oath of allegiance to Georgia. Nine of the 11 either signed the oath or agreed to leave the state. Elizur Butler and Samuel Worcester refused to sign and received sentences of four years' imprisonment and hard labor in the Georgia state prison. Boudinot covered the story in the *Cherokee Phoenix*, and Wirt prepared another case.

The new case was *Worcester v. Georgia*. This time the Cherokee Nation won the case, but Georgia refused to release the missionaries. And Jackson, it was reported, said, "John Marshall has made his decision; now let him enforce it."

Suddenly Cherokee like Major Ridge, his son John Ridge, and Elias Boudinot changed their minds. They felt that the Cherokee had carried their battle as far as they could with the Supreme Court and had won, but that the Court was being ignored by the state of Georgia and the president of the United States. With this continued opposition, they feared the worst if they did not agree to removal. Chief John Ross, however, remained staunch in his insistence on Cherokee rights.

After Georgia divided the Cherokee territory into land lots and gave them out by lottery, Georgians invaded Cherokee country. On December 29, 1835, the Ridges, Boudinot, and others of their thinking met with U.S. negotiators at New Echota to sign a fraudulent treaty. Called the Treaty of New Echota, or sometimes the Removal Treaty, the document was illegal because the signers for the Cherokee Nation were not government officials. They were private Cherokee. Nevertheless, the U.S. Senate ratified the treaty by a single vote. The removal of the Cherokee was now a step closer to happening.

(*Opposite page*) In an effort to drive the Cherokee from the South, the Georgia state government enacted several laws that would strip the Cherokee of their rights. The Cherokee hired a lawyer and brought the case *Cherokee Nation v. Georgia* to the U.S. Supreme Court to fight these laws.

The Trail of Tears

The Georgia lottery winners began to take over the property of the Cherokee living in Georgia. Chief John Ross's home had been confiscated, and he was forced to move his family to Tennessee. Elizur Butler and Samuel Worcester were finally released from the Georgia prison. Worcester decided to go west with the Cherokee who were signing up for emigration. John Walker, who was one of the treaty's supporters, was killed. The Ridges and Elias Boudinot were threatened with death. President Andrew Jackson declared that Ross and his National Council would be held "answerable for every murder committed on the emigrating party."

The fraudulent Treaty of New Echota gave up all Cherokee lands in the east in exchange for $5 million and lands in the west that were partially occupied by the Western Cherokee Nation and partially by the Osage. The treaty also promised that the lands in

In 1838, the Cherokee were removed from Georgia and forced to walk to their new homes in Oklahoma. Moving through harsh climate without adequate clothing or food, thousands lost their lives in the mass migration known as the Trail of Tears.

the west would never be taken by the United States or any state without the consent of the Cherokee.

The deadline for the removal of approximately 15,000 Cherokee was set for two years following the ratification of the treaty, which occurred on May 23, 1836. President Jackson did not recognize any government of the Cherokee in the east. Several hundred pro-treaty Cherokee moved themselves west in 1836 and 1837, but Chief Ross continued to fight the treaty, and thousands of Cherokee stood behind him. They all believed the treaty was fraudulent. General John Ellis Wool, commander of federal troops in the Cherokee Nation, described the situation this way, according to *The Cherokee Nation*:

> The whole scene since I have been in this country has been nothing but a heartrending one, and such a one as I would be glad to get rid of as soon as circumstances will permit. Because I am firm and decided, do not believe I would be unjust. If I could . . . I would remove every Indian tomorrow beyond the reach of the white men, who, like vultures, are watching, ready to pounce upon their prey and strip them of everything they have or expect from the government of the United States. Yes, sir, nineteen-twentieths, if not ninety-nine out of every hundred, will go penniless to the west.

To enforce the removal treaty, stockades were built to hold Cherokee prisoners as they were rounded up. People were dragged from their homes and marched to the prisons to await removal. In an apocryphal story, one such Cherokee, Tsali, was arrested for killing two soldiers as they were taking him and his family from their home. He initially escaped but was later talked into surrendering. Supposedly, he was told that, if he surrendered, the rest of the Cherokee who were hiding out and resisting removal would be left alone. Tsali surrendered and was executed by a firing squad. The remaining Cherokee in the mountains were left alone. For several years after that, they survived by gathering wild foods and hunting. A white man named William Thomas, who had been raised by Cherokee, eventually collected from the government that portion of the money paid for the Cherokee lands that was due to them. With their money, Thomas bought some land that eventually became the Cherokee reservation known as the Qualla Boundary in North Carolina.

The Cherokee at the stockades were imprisoned in a space 200 feet by 500 feet (61 meters by 152 meters), enclosed within 16-foot (5-meter) walls. There was no shelter, no privacy, no provisions for

A Written Account of the Journey

From the Southeast Tennessee Tourism Association pamphlet, Southeast Tennessee Cherokee Native American Guide, Chattanooga, Tennessee, no date:

> Seventeen detachments left from the three main emigrating depots, between June 6 and December 5, 1838. Two of the depots were in Tennessee and the third was eight miles south of Fort Payne, Alabama. The journey took place over various land and water routes and averaged over 1,000 miles. The first three detachments departed from Ross's Landing in June of 1838. They were accompanied by military escorts and were Cherokees captured by the Georgia militia. The first group under Lieutenant Edward Deas left Ross's Landing on June 6 by steamboat. The second group under Captain R.H.K. Whiteley, left Ross's Landing by flatboat on June 12, and the third group under Captain Gus Drane traveled overland from Ross's Landing to Waterloo, Alabama, and from that point traveled by river and land routes to the Indian Territory. Only one other detachment received a military escort, a "pro-treaty" group under John Bell who left the Cherokee Agency on October 10, 1838, and traveled overland through Chattanooga, Memphis, Little Rock before disbanding at Vinyard Post Office, Arkansas on January 7, 1839.

sanitation; the Cherokee slept on the ground. The daily rations were flour and salt pork. Dysentery swept through the camps, and at least 2,000 Cherokee died in the stockades. The Cherokee endured these conditions for as long as two months. Finally, in June 1838,

Chief John Ross, a Cherokee leader, was allowed to supervise the Cherokee Nation's move from Georgia to Oklahoma. After arriving in their new home, Ross attempted to unite the different groups of Cherokee in the region.

5,000 Cherokee were loaded onto steamboats for transportation west. During the hot summer, many people became sick and died.

At this point, John Ross applied and received permission for the Cherokee Nation to take charge of the removal. The first detachment of Cherokee to emigrate under their own leaders

began on August 28, 1838. William Shorey Coodey, a nephew of
John Ross, witnessed the departure of the first detachment. In this
letter, cited in Vicki Rozema's *Voices from the Trail of Tears*, he
wrote about what he saw:

> At noon all was in readiness for moving. The trains were
> stretched out in a line along the road through a heavy forest,
> groups of persons formed about each waggon, others shak-
> ing the hand of some sick friend or relative who would be left
> behind. . . . The day was bright and beautiful, but a gloomy
> thoughtfulness was strongly depicted in the lineaments of every
> face. In all the bustle of preparation there was a silence and still-
> ness of the voice that betrayed the sadness of the heart.
>
> At length the word was given to *move on.* I glanced along
> the line and the form of Going Snake, an aged and respected
> chief whose head eighty winters had whitened, mounted on his
> favorite poney passed before me and lead the way in advance,
> followed by a number of young men on horse back.
>
> At this very moment a low sound of distant thunder fell on
> my ear. In almost an exact western direction a dark spiral cloud
> was rising above the horizon and sent forth a murmur I almost
> fancied a voice of divine indignation for the wrongs of my poor
> and unhappy countrymen, driven by *brutal* power from all they
> loved and cherished in the land of their fathers, to gratify the
> cravings of avarice. The sun was unclouded—no rain fell—the
> thunder rolled away and seemed hushed in the distance. The
> scene around and before me, and in the elements above, were
> peculiarly impressive and singular. It was at once spoken of by
> several persons near me, and looked upon as ominous of some
> future event in the West.
>
> An early severe winter caused much trouble along the way.
> The detachments were trapped by the frozen Mississippi and
> Ohio Rivers in southern Illinois. Without shoes and blankets,
> many became sick and died. A total of about 4,000 died in the
> prisons or along the way. Others ran away. The journal for one
> detachment records runaways every single night along the trail.
> No one knows what became of those people.

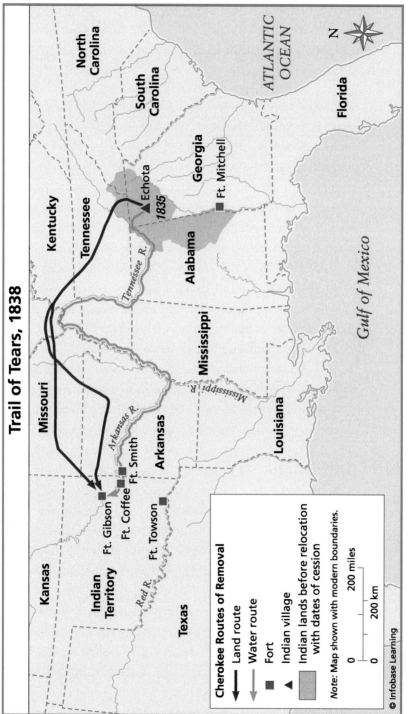

Trail of Tears, 1838

Cherokee Routes of Removal

Land route

Water route

■ Fort

▲ Indian village

Indian lands before relocation
with dates of cession

Note: Map shown with modern boundaries.

0   200 miles

0   200 km

© Infobase Learning

AFTERMATH OF THE TRAIL OF TEARS

When the miserable Trail of Tears had ended, Chief Ross and his followers tried to reestablish the Cherokee Nation in its new home, in what is now northeastern Oklahoma. They sought to bring all the Cherokee back together by reabsorbing the Western Cherokee into the Cherokee Nation, but the Western Cherokee, now known as the Old Settlers, had their own government since at least 1811 and wanted to keep it. The Treaty Party, which consisted of those Cherokee who had backed the Treaty of New Echota, had joined with the Western Cherokee.

In July 1839, Sequoyah and other members of the Western Cherokee met and deposed their chiefs and agreed to rejoin the Cherokee Nation. The next day, Major Ridge, John Ridge, and Elias Boudinot, among the signers of the Treaty of New Echota, were all killed in accordance with the Cherokee constitution, which called for the death penalty for anyone who sold Cherokee land. Members of the Treaty Party and the former Western Cherokee Nation began to retaliate for the killings, and soon, a Cherokee civil war was under way, with killings on both sides escalating.

In May 1842, Stand Watie, a brother of Elias Boudinot, was tried in Arkansas for the killing of James Foreman, who Watie claimed was one of the killers of the three treaty signers. Watie was acquitted on the grounds of self-defense. Then the Starr family raided the home of R.J. Meigs and killed three members of the Ross Party, as the majority was now called. In retaliation, Ross men killed James Starr and one of his sons. John Ross's home took on the appearance of a fortress, with hundreds of armed Cherokee

(Opposite page) After President Andrew Johnson signed the Indian Removal Act in 1830, the Cherokee were forcibly relocated to the Indian Territory west of the Mississippi. The difficult journey became known as the Trail of Tears. This map shows the route of removal and the original land of the Cherokee.

camped around the outskirts to protect the chief and his family from attack. At the same time, Stand Watie established a camp in Arkansas, where he may have been joined by any number of outlaws seeking a safe haven.

This war raged on until 1846, when members of all the factions—the Cherokee Nation, the Western Cherokee Nation, and the Treaty Party—met in Washington for the signing of a new treaty.

The first article of the treaty said "that the lands now occupied by the Cherokee Nation shall be secured to the whole Cherokee people for their common use and benefit." The second article stated that "all difficulties and differences heretofore existing between the several parties of the Cherokee Nation are hereby settled and adjusted, and shall, as far as possible, be forgotten and forever buried in oblivion. All party distinctions shall cease." A general amnesty was declared, pardoning all crimes committed by a Cherokee against another Cherokee or against the Cherokee Nation.

The Civil War and Indian Territory

Following 1846, a tranquility settled over the Cherokee Nation, and the Cherokee made great strides, so much so that many historians have called this period the Golden Age of the Cherokee Nation. Samuel Worcester opened a printing shop that published Cherokee school books and religious tracts. The Cherokee Nation set up its own free, compulsory public school system, with 11 schools and 2 new "seminaries," or high schools, one for young men, the other for young women. It has been said that the public school system was the first of its kind anywhere. A Cherokee orphanage was established, and churches were built. Tahlequah, the capital city, grew; a Supreme Court building was erected there, and Tahlequah also had a Masonic lodge and a strong temperance movement. The newspaper was reestablished, named the *Cherokee Advocate*, and published, as before, in Cherokee and English.

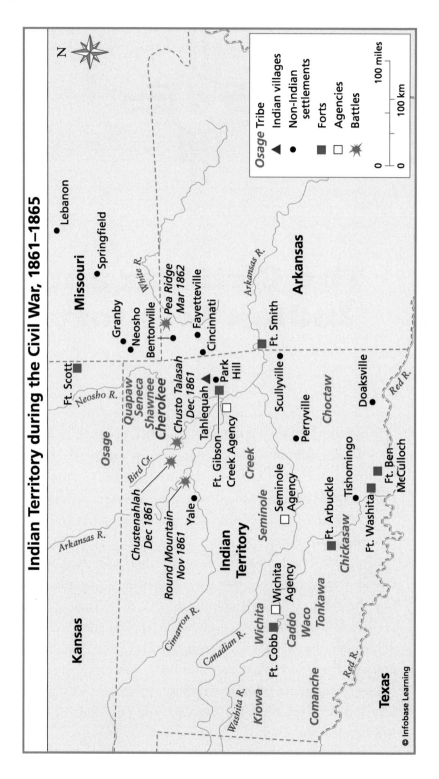

Indian Territory during the Civil War, 1861–1865

Osage Tribe

▲ Indian villages

● Non-Indian settlements

■ Forts

□ Agencies

✳ Battles

100 miles

100 km

0

0

Lebanon

Springfield

Missouri

Granby

Neosho

Bentonville

White R.

Pea Ridge
Mar 1862

Fayetteville

Cincinnati

Ft. Scott

Neosho R.

Quapaw
Seneca
Shawnee
Cherokee

Chusto Talasah
Dec 1861

Park
Hill

Tahlequah

Ft. Gibson
Creek Agency

Creek

Scullyville

Perryville

Choctaw

Doaksville

Red R.

Arkansas

Arkansas R.

Ft. Smith

Osage

Bird Cr.

Chustenahlah
Dec 1861

Round Mountain
Nov 1861

Yale

Arkansas R.

Seminole

Seminole
Agency

Ft. Arbuckle

Chickasaw

Tishomingo

Ft. Washita

Ft. Ben
McCulloch

**Indian
Territory**

Kansas

Cimarron R.

Canadian R.

Wichita

Wichita
Agency

Caddo

Waco

Tonkawa

Ft. Cobb

Kiowa

Washita R.

Comanche

Red R.

Texas

© Infobase Learning

Such times were not to last, however. Many wealthy Cherokee were slave owners and had built fine plantation-style homes. When the Civil War broke out, they sympathized with the South. Chief John Ross strove to keep the Cherokee out of the white man's war, but when his rival Stand Watie agreed to raise Cherokee Confederate forces, Ross reluctantly signed a treaty with the Confederacy. He was trying to keep the Cherokee Nation from dividing. Many Cherokee, however, fought against Watie and his Confederates. When Union forces arrested Chief Ross, he repudiated his Confederate treaty, maintaining that he had been forced to sign it.

Watie fought well for the Confederacy and was promoted to the rank of brigadier general. He became the last Confederate general to surrender, more than two months after Robert E. Lee had surrendered to Ulysses S. Grant at Appomatox, Virginia. With the war at an end, the United States decided to punish the Cherokee Nation for its part in the conflict. The other members of the so-called Five Civilized Tribes (the Creek Nation, the Chickasaw Nation, the Choctaw Nation, and the Seminole Nation) had also had Confederate soldiers. They were punished, too. Land was taken from them, and the remaining lands of the five tribes were combined to create Indian Territory. The former slaves of the Indians were made citizens of the various tribes.

The Eastern Band of Cherokee in North Carolina did not escape involvement in the Civil War. William Thomas gathered a legion of Cherokee for the Confederacy and became known as Colonel Will Thomas. Conley's Sharpshooters, a part of the Thomas Legion, are said to have fired the last shot of the Civil War in North Carolina, near Waynesville.

(Opposite page) This map shows important locations and battles near Indian Territory during the U.S. Civil War.

AFTER THE CIVIL WAR

Shortly after signing the treaty of 1866, which established Indian Territory, Chief Ross died, having served his people for more than 50 years. The Council of the Cherokee Nation appointed William Potter Ross, John Ross's nephew, as chief to fill the vacant post. A year later, Lewis Downing was elected principal chief, and the Cherokee Nation, during the Reconstruction era, began to rebuild and to even improve on what it had had in the past. Much work needed to be done. The Cherokee had lost approximately 5,000 men during the war, leaving one-third of the Cherokee women widows and one-fourth of the children orphans. By 1870, though, the Cherokee Nation was operating 64 public schools, and churches had returned to the territory. A new brick capitol was built in Tahlequah, and the *Cherokee Advocate*, which had suspended publication during the Civil War, began to be printed once again.

Still, progress wasn't being made on all fronts. Indian Territory was becoming a notoriously lawless land, where many criminals went to avoid capture and arrest. Although the tribes had their own lawmen and courts, they were not allowed to arrest white men, so outlaws like the Daltons and Jesse James sought refuge in the territory, or the "Nations" as it was sometimes called. A number of full-blood Cherokee, who were nationalists, were also accused of being outlaws and were hounded by federal law enforcement officers. A federal court was established at Fort Smith, Arkansas, to deal with the lawlessness. It was ruled over by Judge Isaac Parker, who saw it as his duty to save the Indians. This federal court, though, with jurisdiction over Indian Territory, was the source of the worst part of the problem, as the Proctor case demonstrates.

JURISDICTIONAL CONFUSION

In 1872, Zeke Proctor, a Cherokee, went to a place known as Beck's Mill with the intent to kill a white man named Kesterson. Kesterson had been married to one of Proctor's sisters in another part of the

During the U.S. Civil War, the Cherokee Nation splintered into two groups, one of which was led by Stand Watie in support of the Confederacy. When the fighting concluded, leaders from both groups (*above*) negotiated the Treaty of 1866 with the federal government.

Cherokee Nation and had abandoned her along with two small children. Proctor had rescued his sister and her children, taking them to live in his own home. Then Kesterson had moved in with another Cherokee woman at Beck's Mill, near Proctor's home. The insult was too much for him to bear.

At the mill, Proctor confronted Kesterson and shot at him, but the woman Kesterson was living with, Polly Beck, jumped in front of Kesterson and took the bullet. Kesterson ran. Proctor went to the Cherokee sheriff and told him that he had killed a Cherokee woman. The Becks were a prominent Cherokee family, and so were the Proctors. In the meantime, Kesterson had gone to Fort Smith and filed a complaint with U.S. authorities against Proctor for attempted murder of a white man. So there was a clear Cherokee case, the killing of a Cherokee by a Cherokee, and there was a clear case for the U.S. courts, attempted killing of a white man by a Cherokee. There was also the question of whether Kesterson had become a citizen of the Cherokee Nation by marrying a Cherokee woman.

The court at Fort Smith sent some deputies to the Cherokee trial with these instructions. If the Cherokee court found Proctor guilty of murder and sentenced him to hang, then the deputies were to just return home. All was well. If the court let Proctor go, the deputies were to arrest him on the federal charge and bring him back to Fort Smith.

The day of the trial, when the Beck family arrived, Zeke Proctor's brother, Johnson, blocked the door. The Becks were heavily armed. When Johnson confronted them, the Becks opened fire, killing Johnson, who was unarmed. Both sides commenced firing, and when the gun battle was all over, nine men were killed and two more were mortally wounded. A number of others had received minor wounds, and Zeke Proctor had run away. The Cherokee Nation issued warrants for the arrests of the Becks, while the U.S. court at Fort Smith issued warrants for the arrest of Zeke Proctor, the judge, and even Johnson Proctor, who was dead.

The United States asked Chief Downing for help in capturing Zeke Proctor, but Downing refused. The court at Fort Smith was just about ready to ask for troops from Fort Sill when cooler heads prevailed, and a general amnesty was proclaimed. Zeke Proctor went on to become a sheriff of an Arkansas county. This story is just one example of the jurisdictional confusion that existed in Indian Territory during those years.

OKLAHOMA

The land to the immediate west of Indian Territory was opened to whites in 1889 and organized as the Oklahoma Territory. Just as had happened in Georgia, the Cherokee Nation was being surrounded by white people.

In 1887, the U.S. Congress passed the General Allotment Act, more commonly known as the Dawes Act after the sponsor of the bill, Senator Henry Dawes. The Dawes Act was passed to make

In 1889, the federal government held its first land run in Oklahoma Territory and offered plots of land to settlers on a first-come basis. Although these land runs helped Oklahoma achieve statehood, it also led to the dismantling of Cherokee government and society.

Indians individual landowners. Before then, tribes held land in common. The new law granted 160 acres of land to each head of a family, 80 acres to each single person over age 18 and each orphan, and 40 acres to each single person under age 18. A deed for the land would be issued to each owner, but the U.S. government restricted the land for 25 years—meaning the owner could not sell or lease the land without federal permission. Once the allotments were issued, any remaining tribal land would be made available to whites.

At first, the Cherokee and the other tribes in Indian Territory were exempt from the Dawes Act by treaty. In 1893, however, Congress established a Dawes Commission to deal with allotment in Indian Territory. Three years later, the power of determining citizenship was taken from the Cherokee Nation and given to the Dawes Commission. In 1898, the Curtis Act was passed, giving U.S. courts the power to determine the membership of the tribes in Indian Territory. The act declared that when the citizenship rolls of the tribes were complete, the Dawes Commission would be able to begin to allot the lands. While the Cherokee had tried to fight the Curtis Act, they were finally forced to negotiate with the Dawes Commission.

An agreement was reached in 1900 declaring that the rolls compiled by the Dawes Commission would be the final rolls. The agreement said that "the government of the Cherokee Nation shall not continue longer than March 4, 1906, subject to future legislation as Congress may deem proper," and it said that all Cherokee citizens would become citizens of the United States. The commission then began its work to compile the rolls. It was the commissioners who determined who was Cherokee and who was not. It was the commissioners who decided how much Cherokee blood an individual had. In many cases, when an individual had white or African-American blood in addition to Cherokee blood, the commissioners just decided based on appearance whether that individual was Cherokee or African American or white. They changed people's names in some cases.

While the Cherokee Nation was supposed to have been dissolved by March 1906, the allotment process was so complex and time consuming that the dissolution date was extended until June 1914. As it was, Chief William C. Rogers continued in office until 1917 to sign the deeds of land transfer.

In the meantime, Oklahoma Territory and Indian Territory were combined to form the new state of Oklahoma on November 16, 1907. Will Rogers once said, "We had the greatest territory in the world, and they ruined it when they made a state." He was right. The Cherokee fared much worse under statehood than they had under their own government. By the time of Oklahoma statehood, the Cherokee Nation had produced more college graduates than had the states of Arkansas and Texas combined, but by the time of the 1970 census, a mere 63 years later, the average adult Cherokee had but four years of school. Though many Cherokee of mixed blood became active immediately in state politics, most of the full-blood Cherokee retreated to the back hills and did their best to live traditional lives and ignore the state of Oklahoma and the teeming white population around them.

The Three Tribes

While the Cherokee Nation was not totally destroyed in 1907, it was effectively put to sleep. The president of the United States began to appoint the chiefs of the Cherokee Nation. Many of them were chiefs just long enough to sign some documents. Thus they became known as the "chiefs for a day." There was no council. There were no elections.

THE CHEROKEE NATION

The Cherokee, though, were not politically inactive. Several grassroots Cherokee political organizations existed over the years. In 1941, these organizations combined forces and elected Jesse Bartley Milam as principal chief. The election, of course, was not recognized by the United States, but in a remarkable development, President Franklin Roosevelt "rubber-stamped" the election by appointing Milam as chief. So at the same time, Milam was an elected chief as well as another in the long list of appointed chiefs. The other remarkable aspect of Milam's appointment was that it was for one year. He was reappointed after that and remained chief until his death in 1949. During those years, Milam worked

Elected in 1987 and again in 1991, Wilma Mankiller became the first female chief of the Cherokee Nation. Above, Mankiller receives the Presidential Medal of Freedom from President Bill Clinton.

to preserve the Cherokee language, secure land for a Cherokee Heritage Center, and push for Cherokee claims against the U.S. government.

After Milam's death, W.W. "Bill" Keeler was appointed chief by President Harry Truman, and Keeler remained in office until 1975, when Ross Swimmer was elected principal chief. The Cherokee Nation had been given the right to elect its chiefs again in 1971, and Keeler was actually an elected chief for one term. Swimmer served for 10 years, resigning to become the head of the Bureau of Indian Affairs. Wilma Mankiller, who had been his deputy chief, served out his term and then was twice elected, serving also for 10 years. Under the Mankiller administration, the Cherokee Nation's new justice department was established, including a marshal's service and a court with a tribal prosecutor. A cross-deputization agreement was signed between the Cherokee Nation and the sheriffs of Cherokee and other counties

From Principal Chief Wilma Mankiller's 1990 Inauguration Address

"It's a fine time for celebration because as we approach the twenty-first century, the Cherokee Nation still has a strong, viable tribal government. Not only do we have a government that has continued to exist, we have a tribal government that's growing and progressing and getting stronger. We've managed not to just barely hang on, we've managed to move forward in a very strong, very affirmative way. Given our history of adversity, I think it's a testament to our tenacity, both individually and collectively as a people, that we've been able to keep the Cherokee Nation government going since time immemorial."

in Oklahoma, and a Cherokee Nation Code conforming with Oklahoma's statutes was adopted.

In 1995, Chief Mankiller was replaced by Joe Byrd, whose term was plagued with controversy. The trouble began before the election. Byrd's toughest opponent was George Bearpaw, who was Mankiller's choice to succeed her. In the primary, Bearpaw came in first, followed by Byrd and then attorney Chad Smith. Bearpaw, though, had to face Byrd in a runoff since he did not receive enough votes to win outright. Just after the primary, however, it was discovered that Bearpaw had been convicted of a felony years before, making him ineligible to run for office, according to the Cherokee Nation constitution. Bearpaw maintained that he was eligible, as his record had been expunged. The Judicial Appeals Tribunal, the highest court in the Cherokee Nation, however, said that he had failed to disclose his conviction when he signed up to run for office, and because of this, he was declared ineligible. Smith petitioned the tribunal to postpone the runoff and have new ballots printed with his and Byrd's names on them. The tribunal declared that the runoff would proceed with the ballots as printed but that no votes for Bearpaw would count. So Byrd was elected.

While Byrd was chief, a council member attempted to gain access to some tribal financial records. The council member was refused. The records are supposed to be public documents and certainly should not have been denied to a council member. She went to the judicial tribunal. The tribunal issued a search warrant and gave it to the marshal's service. Marshals, with the warrant, went to the tribal offices and made copies of the records. Byrd was out of town. When he returned, he fired all of the marshals and tried to have the judges impeached. He hired a new group of marshals and had them take over the historic council house, which was then being used as a courthouse and offices for the judges.

The word spread quickly, and by the next morning, a great crowd of interested Cherokee gathered around the council house in downtown Tahlequah, Oklahoma. The fired marshals were there. An attempt was made to retake the council house, during which some people were injured. The attempt failed, but the whole event was widely publicized. The Cherokee Nation was in the news once again.

In a court proceeding held by eight members of the tribal council, the three-member judicial tribunal was impeached. The next day the justices said the court proceeding was illegal because the council failed to meet a quorum as called for by the tribe's constitution. The justices vowed to stay in office.

Byrd and the majority of the tribal council, however, called the impeachments final and said they would not recognize orders or decisions coming from the former tribunal members. The tribunal issued arrest warrants for Byrd and Deputy Chief J. Garland Eagle because they did not appear for a court hearing.

Because the Cherokee marshals were under a restraining order, the tribunal asked the Bureau of Indian Affairs to carry out the arrests, but the BIA officers informed the tribunal that they would submit the order to the solicitor's office of the Department of the Interior to "determine if the orders are valid."

Despite all the turmoil, the issue was never resolved. Chief Byrd remained in office for his full four-year term. He was then defeated by Chad Smith, who seems to have let the whole matter just fade away.

The 1866 treaty following the Civil War not only abolished slavery in the Cherokee Nation but also made all the former slaves of Cherokees into citizens of the Cherokee Nation. Later that same year, the Cherokee Nation amended its constitution to declare the "freedmen" to be citizens. Despite those two actions, in 2007, the Cherokee Nation held a national election and voted to restrict tribal citizenship to those individuals who were descended from Indians listed by blood on the Dawes Commission roll, thereby excluding the descendants of the freedmen. Chad Smith has seemed to be in support of this move, maintaining that the vote was an act of tribal sovereignty and that no one has the right to determine Cherokee

Nation citizenship but the citizens themselves. Many Cherokee, apparently, agree with him. But the Descendants of Freedmen of the Five Civilized Tribes took the issue to court. In January 2011, a Cherokee Nation district court judge ruled that the 2007 vote violated the 1866 treaty. After the ruling, the tribe was considering its options, including a possible appeal.

Chief Smith was also instrumental in establishing the first independent Cherokee newspaper and in greatly increasing Cherokee Nation gaming operations. He has challenged the U.S. government a number of times in the area of tribal sovereignty.

THE EASTERN BAND OF CHEROKEE INDIANS

The Treaty of 1819 stipulated that any Cherokee head of a family could remain in the East by applying for a 640-acre reservation and becoming a U.S. citizen. Forty-nine Cherokee registered under this provision and settled in the mountains in North Carolina. Yonaguska and Euchella were among them. Most of them eventually settled near the junction of Soco Creek and the Oconaluftee River, a place later called Quallatown. Yonaguska, or Drowning Bear, was their chief. They were known as the Oconaluftee, or Luftee, or Qualla Indians. In 1831, William Holland Thomas, known to them as Wil Usdi, meaning Little Will, became their legal counsel. Yonaguska had adopted Thomas as a youth, and he knew the Cherokee well.

Even the infamous Treaty of New Echota of 1835, the Removal treaty, reaffirmed the rights of the Qualla Indians to remain in the East. Article 12 of that treaty said that a Cherokee could stay if he was qualified and was willing to come under state law.

During the time of Removal, when the Cherokee named Tsali killed two soldiers and became a fugitive, Will Thomas was afraid that the conflict might jeopardize the security of the Qualla Indians. Thomas, therefore, offered his assistance to the army. He enlisted Euchella and other Qualla Indians to help him, and they captured Tsali, who was executed. Almost immediately after the execution, it was announced that Removal had officially ended. The legend of Tsali grew, but the status of the Qualla Indians remained uncertain. Other Cherokee came under Article 12 until the population grew to around 1,400.

Yonaguska died in 1839, and afterward, Will Thomas became the de facto chief of the Qualla Cherokee. He worked tirelessly on their behalf in Washington. He managed to collect some of the money due them for the sale of their lands, and with that money, he purchased land in Western North Carolina for them to live on. The land was registered in his name. The largest tract became known as the Qualla Boundary. To protect this property for his clients, Thomas organized the Cherokee Company and had it approved by the governor of the state in 1847. The stated purpose of the company was to produce silk and sugar, but little of that was done. Thomas did, however, transfer some of the lands he had purchased for the Qualla Indians to the name of the company.

Over the years, several attempts were made to complete the removal of the Cherokee by forcing the Quallatown Cherokee to join those in the West, but none of these efforts worked. By 1855, the Quallatown Cherokee, with much help from Thomas, had won the right to remain in North Carolina permanently. A census had enumerated more than 2,000 Cherokee living in Quallatown and other areas of the East.

Thomas was working hard to get North Carolina to admit that the Cherokee were citizens of the state. Toward that end he always exaggerated their progress. He overstated their literacy rates and their Christianity. In actuality, they were mostly subsistence farmers, eking out a meager living on small farms by growing corn, potatoes, beans, wheat, and some orchard fruits. The small Christian population among them was growing. They lived in small log cabins like their white neighbors. Most, however, did not speak English, and almost none could read, either English or Cherokee.

They retained many of their old, traditional customs, paramount among them the ballplay and the green corn dance. They dressed more colorfully than their white neighbors did, with the men still wearing turbans and hunting jackets.

By the time of the outbreak of the Civil War, Thomas had become a member of the North Carolina legislature, and he had voted for secession. With the war under way, he organized a Cherokee Legion for the Confederacy. For most of the war, it was stationed in upper East Tennessee. In *The Eastern Band of Cherokees: 1819–1900*, John Finger writes that "approximately 400 Cherokees served in the Legion at one time or another, representing most of the able-bodied men of the Band." By 1863 and 1864, the Cherokee were practically starving. Not surprisingly, Unionists and Union newspapers depicted the Cherokee Confederates as bloodthirsty savages who were scalping Union soldiers and violating Union women. Thomas surrendered the legion in May 1865, gaining permission for its soldiers to retain their weapons for hunting. Thomas was 60 years old, deeply in debt, and showing signs of mental weakness.

Immediately following the Civil War, there was an outbreak of smallpox among the Cherokee in North Carolina, and before it had run its course, 125 Indians had died. Thomas had more mental problems, and George Bushyhead became the leader of the Eastern Band, making many trips to Washington on its behalf. The members of the Eastern Band were destitute following the war. Their crops were in ruin. They were living in extreme poverty, nearly starving. Drunkenness was a major problem.

In 1868, the U.S. Congress at last recognized the Eastern Band as a distinct tribe. There were more attempts to get the North Carolina Cherokee to move west and join the Cherokee Nation. There were swindles. Most of the land they lived on was still in the name of Will Thomas, and some of it was eventually sold to pay his debts. In 1870 Flying Squirrel was elected principal chief of the Eastern Band. In 1871 and 1872, more than 125 Eastern Cherokee

Ayunini (*right, behind woman*), also know as Swimmer, was a Cherokee dedicated to the culture and traditions of his tribe. When anthropologist James Mooney came to North Carolina to study the Cherokee, much of his information came from Ayunini.

voluntarily moved to the Cherokee Nation in the west. After two lawsuits and arbitration, and the payment of some money owed to the Eastern Band by the federal government, the land issue was finally settled with title to the Qualla Boundary and 15,000 acres outside the boundary held in trust for the Eastern Band by the Bureau of Indian Affairs.

In 1880, Yellow Hill, later to be called Cherokee, became the seat of government for the Eastern Band, and Nimrod Jarret Smith became the chief. That year, another 161 Eastern Cherokee moved to the Cherokee Nation. The legal status of the Cherokee in North

Carolina was still in question. They paid state taxes and voted, but North Carolina was still hesitant to actually call them citizens. They were sometimes called wards of the U.S. government.

In 1887, James Mooney went to North Carolina to conduct field research among the Cherokee there. He had met Chief Smith two years earlier in Washington. His main informant became Swimmer, or Ayunini, a traditionalist. Mooney even visited Will Thomas, who by this time was confined to a mental institution. In 1891, Smith was defeated and replaced by Stilwell Saunook. Nimrod Smith and William Holland Thomas both died in 1893, Swimmer died in 1899, and in 1900 James Mooney published his *Myths of the Cherokee*.

According to John R. Finger in *Cherokee Americans*, "Western North Carolina was only gradually emerging from its geographic isolation in 1900." Full-scale commercial exploitation of Cherokee timber had begun in 1890, and that continued to provide most of the tribal income into the twentieth century. Schools were built, and in 1916, so was a small, modern hospital. By 1911, Cherokee basket makers were selling their wares in Asheville. In 1914, the first Cherokee Fair was organized. It provided an outlet for Cherokee artisans and attracted white visitors to the reservation. It also became an annual event.

Following the Selective Service Act of 1917, 115 Cherokee registered for the draft. Sixty-eight Eastern Cherokee served in the U.S. armed forces during World War I. Following the war there was a movement to divide the Cherokee land holdings into allotments and to dissolve the government of the Eastern Band. The battle raged on until 1930, when the Eastern Band's tribal council voted unanimously to reject the idea. Perhaps they had taken note of the disastrous effects of allotment on the Cherokee Nation, now in the state of Oklahoma. In addition, another reason for their rejection was the confusing legal status of Eastern Band tribal members. They had sometimes been allowed to vote and sometimes not. The issue wasn't even resolved when

James Mooney on Ayunini (Swimmer)

"Born about 1835, shortly before the Removal, [Swimmer] grew up under the instruction of masters to be a priest, doctor, and keeper of tradition, so that he was recognized as an authority throughout the band and by such a competent outside judge as Colonel Thomas. He served through the [Civil War] as second sergeant of the Cherokee Company A, Sixty-ninth North Carolina Confederate Infantry, Thomas Legion. He was prominent in the local affairs of the [Eastern] [B]and, and no Green-corn dance, ballplay, or other tribal function was ever considered complete without his presence and active assistance. A genuine aboriginal antiquarian and patriot, proud of his people and their ancient system, he took delight in recording in his native alphabet the songs and sacred formulas of priests and dancers and the names of medicinal plants and the prescriptions with which they were compounded, while his mind was a storehouse of Indian tradition. . . . He spoke no English, and to the day of his death clung to the moccasin and the turban, together with the rattle, his badge of authority. He died in March, 1899, aged about sixty-five, and was buried like a true Cherokee on the slope of a forest-clad mountain. Peace to his ashes and sorrow for his going, for with him perished half the tradition of a people."

Source: James Mooney, *Myths of the Cherokee*

Congress passed the Indian Citizenship Act of 1924, which made all Native Americans citizens of the United States. Despite the new law, North Carolina voter registration officials continued to deny Eastern Band members the right to vote by refusing to register them.

Although the timber industry went into a decline in the early twentieth century, several other things happened that were fortunate for the Eastern Band. There was a renewed interest in tourism in Western North Carolina, and a renewed interest in the Cherokee. Around the same time, a major highway program came into being. The Great Smoky Mountains National Park was established in 1934. Also in the 1930s, when President Franklin Roosevelt appointed John Collier as commissioner of Indian affairs, traditional Cherokee crafts received another big boost. Collier encouraged traditional crafts as well as traditional ceremonies.

The creation of Great Smoky Mountains National Park, the helpfulness of the Collier administration, renewed national interest in Native Americans, and a conscious push for tourism by the Eastern Band, which included Cherokees dressing up like Plains Indians, all worked to attract tourists to the Qualla Boundary. Tourism grew on the reservation, with many leases going to white people. Tourist shops and motels were built. Business slowed almost to a stop, however, when the United States entered World War II. Many Cherokee found employment in war-related industries, and many young men joined the services.

When the war ended, Cherokee in North Carolina were still unable to register to vote, but the war had changed many Cherokee. They were no longer simply willing to take it. A great organized effort finally resulted in success, and in 1946, the Cherokee were at last able to register to vote. Sales of Indian craft items increased dramatically around the same time.

In 1950, *Unto These Hills*, a play dramatizing Cherokee history, premiered in a new outdoor theater in Cherokee, North Carolina. The play has been an enormous success, with more than 6 million people having seen it as of 2010. In 1952, the Oconaluftee Indian Village and the Museum of the Cherokee Indian were added to the major tourist attractions in the town of Cherokee. The U.S. government, however, was in a new mode. It was ready to terminate the federal-tribal relationship. Throughout the rest of the 1950s, the

Eastern Band was involved in protecting itself from Termination. In the end, the band was successful.

During the 1960s, the North Carolina Cherokee prospered, with their developing tourism, with President Lyndon Johnson's "Great Society" social reforms, and with help from a number of federal agencies. The Eastern Band became the first American Indian tribe to pay for its own police and to establish its own sanitation and fire departments. In 1975, Congress passed the Indian Self-Determination and Education Assistance Act. The Eastern Band had already been practicing such self-determination on its own.

In 1982, the Eastern Band began to sponsor a large bingo operation, bringing in thousands of dollars. In 2002, Harrah's Cherokee Casino opened, and the casino business has been a major economic boost to the reservation community.

Under the administration of Chief Michell Hicks, the Eastern Band is currently involved in language preservation, with a Cherokee language immersion program, as well as adult Cherokee language classes. These programs are conducted with the cooperation of Western Carolina University's Cherokee language program.

THE UNITED KEETOOWAH BAND OF CHEROKEE INDIANS

The U.S. Congress recognized the United Keetoowah Band of Cherokee Indians (UKB) in 1946. The band's constitution, by-laws, and corporate charter were ratified in 1950. The UKB in Oklahoma was established because the Cherokee Nation was dormant and its chiefs were being appointed by the U.S. president. Jim Pickup was the first chief of the United Keetoowah Band, serving from 1946 to 1954.

There has been much confusion because of the name of the band. The UKB is often mistakenly thought to be the same as the Keetoowah Society, but it is not. The Keetoowah Society is an old traditionalist society of Cherokee, dating back at least to the American Civil War, perhaps farther back. The Keetoowah Band is

Since establishing the Oconaluftee Indian village and the Museum of the Cherokee Indian in 1952, the Eastern Band of Cherokee in North Carolina have used tourism to help support their community.

a political organization, a federally recognized Indian tribe. They are two separate organizations, though some of the confusion perhaps stems from the fact that, in the early days, many people belonged to both groups.

In the 1940s, it was widely believed that the Cherokee Nation would soon be a victim of the federal Termination policy, and many in the Keetoowah Band felt that it would be the obvious inheritor of responsibility for the Cherokee in Oklahoma.

Throughout the 1950s and into the '60s, the status of the Keetoowah Band was in a constant state of fluctuation. One moment, the band was told that it could not do anything without the permission of Bill Keeler, the presidentially appointed chief of the Cherokee Nation, and the next, it was told that it did not need his permission. The band was told that it did not represent the Cherokee tribe.

Georgia Rae Leeds, in *The United Keetoowah Band of Cherokee Indians in Oklahoma*, writes, "The Band was a victim of ambiguous federal policy. On the one hand, the government gave the Keetoowahs a charter enabling them to construct an economic program for the members, while on the other it froze the monies. The federal government weakened the organization and then federal officials dismissed the Band for being weak."

In the early 1960s, two attempts were made to locate industries in the Cherokee territory of Oklahoma, with the Keetoowah Band as a beneficiary. Both failed. But 40 acres adjacent to the Sequoyah Training School were acquired. Earl Boyd Pierce was the attorney for both the Keetoowah Band and the Cherokee Nation, and he managed to get the land placed in the name of the Cherokee Tribe of Oklahoma. With the business ventures a dead issue, it was decided to set aside 10 acres for an arts and crafts training center, a parking area, and a gas station. The Keetoowah Band also wanted a council house. At a dedication ceremony upon completion of the project, neither Chief Keeler nor anyone else acknowledged the part the Keetoowah Band played in the process.

For the next 11 years, the Keetoowah Band was engaged in disputed elections, federal grand jury indictments, and political infighting. Bill Glory was appointed chief to fill out the term of Jim Pickup, who had died. Glory got along well with Chief Keeler for a time. In 1969, however, Glory moved out of the office in the new complex, thereby giving up the Keetoowah Band's claims to the place. For the next several years, Chief Glory failed to call elections. When he called a council meeting, the council members did not show up, or when the council called a meeting, Glory did not show up. It was not until 1978 that another election was held, and in that election, Jim Gordon was chosen chief.

Chief Gordon guided the band into applying for a grant under the 1975 Indian Self-Determination and Education Assistance Act. The band created a housing authority. The Bureau of Indian Affairs had decided that the Keetoowah Band had all the same rights and privileges as the Cherokee Nation, but when Chief Ross Swimmer threatened a Cherokee Nation lawsuit against the bureau, it changed its position. For the rest of his administration, Chief Gordon battled with Chief Swimmer over the rights and the status of the Keetoowah Band.

In 1982, John Hair was elected chief of the United Keetoowah Band. Since the Bureau of Indian Affairs had continually refused to fund the band because of dual membership with the Cherokee Nation and the likelihood that the same people would be receiving money twice, Chief Hair applied for a grant to separate the Keetoowah Band's roll from that of the Cherokee Nation. In 1985, Chief Swimmer went to Washington as head of the Bureau of Indian Affairs. Swimmer's successor as chief of the Cherokee Nation, Wilma Mankiller, continued his policies toward the Keetoowah Band.

In an attempt to put some money in the coffers, Chief Hair authorized the licensing of smoke shops. Toward that end, he created the United Keetoowah Band Enterprise Board. In 1990, the band purchased a building in Tahlequah for its first bingo hall and established offices in the basement. It had also licensed 22 smoke shops. The band opened a second bingo operation in Sperry, Oklahoma. The state of Oklahoma, however, closed the Sperry bingo operation.

The smoke shops created a fury in Vian, Oklahoma, where local merchants complained that they were facing unfair business practices. Smoke shops owned by Native Americans and on Indian land are not required to collect state tobacco taxes. One shop was vandalized and later burned. The city council ordered the fire department to stay away. The police in Vian arrested a BIA employee thinking that he was a Keetoowah Band member.

Then more trouble came from the Cherokee Nation, which decided that it had the power to tax cigarettes in Keetoowah Band smoke shops. When the shop owners refused to pay, Mankiller ordered raids on the shops. At one shop, deputies held guns on two female employees, handcuffed them, and took them to jail. Rough tactics were also used at other shops. Violence was threatened. Mankiller said that if the shop owners were not stopped, a civil war could follow. The United Keetoowah Band took its case to court and lost. The courts determined that while the band is a federally recognized tribe, it does not have jurisdiction over any Indian land. The licensing and taxing of smoke shops by the Cherokee Nation was upheld.

Not all the news was bad, though. The band succeeded in separating its membership from that of the Cherokee Nation, and in the 1990 election, the Cherokee Nation attempted to run a slate of its own candidates, called the Reformed Keetoowahs, for Keetoowah Band positions. None of them were elected.

John Ross was the next Keetoowah chief. Much of his energy was spent in defending the sovereignty of the band. Chief Mankiller and some of her allies in the U.S. Congress made several attempts to terminate the band. Ross was also busy trying to acquire land for the band. Because of interference from the Cherokee Nation, in league with the Bureau of Indian Affairs, the band decided to look outside of Oklahoma. Tennessee and North Carolina were considered, along with Arkansas. The closest the band came to obtaining land was in 1994 when Wanda Gray donated four or five acres of land in Waldron, Arkansas, to the band. Plans were made to relocate there, but they never quite materialized.

Other improvements came, however, as the Keetoowah Band expanded its bingo operation into a full-fledged casino and began to make money. The Bureau of Indian Affairs also changed its position. The band began to receive federal funds. It constructed a new office building and began to operate a number of tribal programs. The band puts on its own annual holiday, which has begun to rival, and even outdo, the Cherokee National Holiday held by the Cherokee Nation. Under the leadership of Principal Chief George Wickliffe, a bilingual Cherokee, the Keetoowah Band is heavily involved in Cherokee language programs and in teaching Cherokee language classes. In addition, a number of social service and early childhood education services are available. The Keetoowah Band has become more involved with the Eastern Band in various ways, having made several trips to Cherokee, North Carolina. Chief Wickliffe has been very vocal in support of the efforts of the Eastern Band to stop Duke Energy from building a power station near the sacred site of Keetoowah. As of October 2010, Duke Energy officials had agreed to move the power station to respect Cherokee demands, another example of Cherokee efforts to defend their sovereignty.

The Cherokee
Today

The Cherokee today are divided into three federally recognized tribes: the Cherokee Nation, headquartered in Tahlequah, Oklahoma; the Eastern Band of Cherokee Indians, based on a reservation in North Carolina known as the Qualla Boundary; and the United Keetoowah Band of Cherokee Indians, also based in Tahlequah, Oklahoma. In addition there are many groups of people calling themselves Cherokee in various places around the country and even outside of the country, in Mexico. Tony Mack McClure in *Cherokee Proud* has identified 250 such "Cherokee" groups.

The Cherokee Nation today has approximately 260,000 registered tribal members. While many reside in the historic Cherokee Nation (all or parts of 14 counties in northeast Oklahoma), most live in other places all over the country and the world. Some are affiliated with organized Cherokee communities in such places as Dallas and Houston, Texas; Albuquerque, New Mexico;

Sacramento and Los Angeles, California; and even New York City. With the population of the Eastern Band (12,500) and the United Keetoowah Band (16,000) considered, the total Cherokee population is close to 300,000, and that is not taking into consideration any of the other groups or individuals who claim Cherokee blood.

There are Cherokee in all walks of life. Bud Adams, the owner of the Tennessee Titans football team, is a registered citizen of the Cherokee Nation, as are film actors Clu Gulager and Wes Studi. There are Cherokee politicians and writers. Barbara McAlister is an internationally known opera singer. There are Cherokee working in

There are thousands of Cherokee throughout the United States, many of whom study traditional Cherokee language and customs. A principal chief leads the Cherokee Nation and its members. Above, Principal Chief Chad Smith delivers a speech in 2004.

bookstores and restaurants. There are Cherokee teachers from preschool to universities. There are amateur and professional athletes.

Of those roughly 300,000 Cherokee, only a small percentage speak the Cherokee language or lead anything like a traditional Cherokee life. Most live like regular Americans. Some read books to learn what they can about Cherokee culture and traditions, and many travel to Oklahoma or to North Carolina to take advantage of the celebratory holidays, visit the museums, and purchase Cherokee crafts to take home. Many attend churches and have jobs like other Americans have. Many attend colleges and universities. Many are actually more "white" by blood than Cherokee. But they all have one thing in common. They are fiercely Cherokee, and many would argue with anyone who tried to tell them they are not Cherokee.

But the minority, the mostly full-blood, Cherokee-speaking people, still attend stomp dances and sing the old songs. Many of them are craftspeople, making pots, baskets, bows and arrows, and blow guns. Many of them attend Cherokee language churches, mostly Baptist or Methodist. Some speak the Cherokee language in their homes. They are the core of the Cherokee people. Principal Chief Chad Smith, in his November 12, 1999, progress report, wrote:

> What greater gift can we give our children than the sense of identity, the knowledge and strength of our ancestors and the inspiration to live good lives? What greater service can we provide to our citizens than cultural education? It is such an important duty that our elected officials are obligated by the constitution to swear an oath to do everything within their power to promote the language and culture.
>
> The principles and wisdom of our culture, clearly, are the driving forces that have allowed us, as a people, to face adversity, survive, adapt, prosper, and excel. It is equally clear that these same principles, wisdom, and sense of identity will keep our children in school, off drugs and alcohol, and make them resilient as they grow into happy, productive adults.

The power and spirit of our tribe is its culture. It is the richness of that culture that will allow our children to be strong, proud, and fulfilled.

The Cherokee Nation, the Eastern Band of Cherokee Indians, and the United Keetoowah Band of Cherokee Indians all operate casinos, bringing much-needed capital into the tribes. The money generated by these gaming establishments is added to the money that the tribes receive from the federal government for programs, and this revenue allows the tribes to provide even more programs and services to the Cherokee people. The outlook is pretty good right now for the Cherokee, but knowing the history of the U.S. government's vacillating policies, the Cherokee must always remain vigilant.

Chronology

1540	Hernando de Soto enters Cherokee country at Guasili and Canasoga.
1673	Virginians James Needham and Gabriel Arthur visit the Cherokee.
1681	Cherokee are sold as slaves in South Carolina.
1711–1713	The Cherokee and the English of Charlestown, South Carolina, drive the Tuscarora out of the Southeast. The Cherokee receive guns from Charlestown for this purpose.

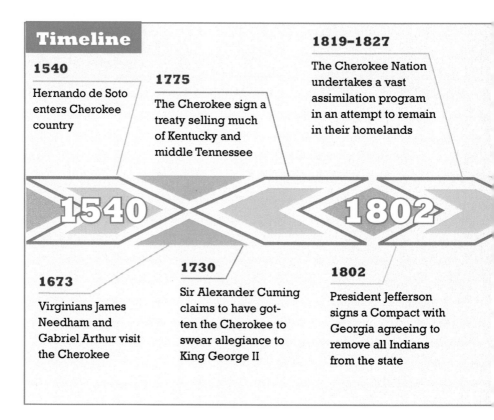

Timeline

1540

Hernando de Soto enters Cherokee country

1775

The Cherokee sign a treaty selling much of Kentucky and middle Tennessee

1819–1827

The Cherokee Nation undertakes a vast assimilation program in an attempt to remain in their homelands

1673

Virginians James Needham and Gabriel Arthur visit the Cherokee

1730

Sir Alexander Cuming claims to have gotten the Cherokee to swear allegiance to King George II

1802

President Jefferson signs a Compact with Georgia agreeing to remove all Indians from the state

1715   Some Cherokee join the Yamassee and the Catawba to fight against Charlestown.

1716   The Cherokee make peace with Charlestown.

1721   Thirty-seven Cherokee meet with Governor Nicolson of Charlestown and agree to name one Cherokee to deal with Charlestown in matters of trade. They name Wrosetaseto. The English agree to do the same and name George Chicken. The Cherokee cede a tract of land to the Charlestown colony.

1730   Sir Alexander Cuming visits the Cherokee town of Keowee and claims to have gotten the Cherokee to swear allegiance to King George II. Cuming names Moytoy "emperor of the Cherokees" and takes seven Cherokee back to England with him.

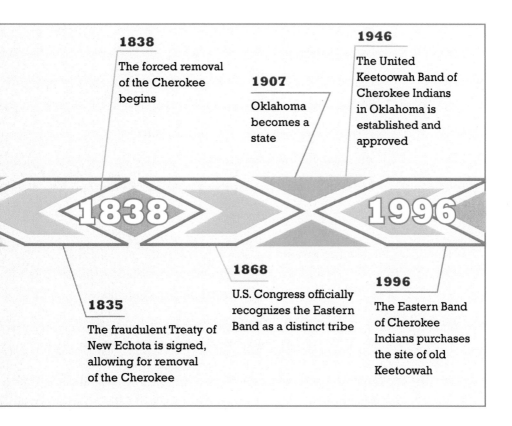

1838
The forced removal of the Cherokee begins

1907
Oklahoma becomes a state

1946
The United Keetoowah Band of Cherokee Indians in Oklahoma is established and approved

1835
The fraudulent Treaty of New Echota is signed, allowing for removal of the Cherokee

1868
U.S. Congress officially recognizes the Eastern Band as a distinct tribe

1996
The Eastern Band of Cherokee Indians purchases the site of old Keetoowah

1736	Christian Gottlieb Priber, a Jesuit priest, moves into Cherokee country and attempts to turn the Cherokee Nation into a communist state.
1738	Smallpox hits the Cherokee.
1739	The English capture Priber, who dies in prison.
1756–1759	Cherokee who had agreed to fight the Shawnees, French allies, are attacked by Virginians, who kill 24 of them. Cherokee respond by killing 24 settlers. Soldiers under Colonel Montgomery destroy Cherokee towns.
1760	Cherokee lay siege to Fort Loudon and force its surrender.
1761	Colonel James Grant and 2,000 men invade Cherokee country and destroy 15 towns; Ada gal'kala signs peace treaties with South Carolina and Virginia.
1775	The Cherokee sign a treaty with the Transylvania Land Company at Sycamore Shoals, selling much of Kentucky and middle Tennessee. Dragging Canoe protests.
1776	Cherokee attack illegal settlers known as Wataugans.
1777	Dragging Canoe and his followers move their towns and become known as Chickamaugans.
1792	Dragging Canoe dies.
1794	The Chickamaugans sign a treaty.
1802	President Thomas Jefferson signs a Compact with Georgia agreeing to remove all Indians from the state as soon as is practical.
1817–1827	Cherokee government is reorganized with a principal chief, a bicameral legislature, a judicial tribunal, eight judicial districts, elections, and a written constitution.
1819	A treaty provides that a Cherokee head of family could remain in ceded territory by applying for a 640-acre reservation and becoming a citizen of the United States. Those who do so become the nucleus of the Eastern Band of Cherokees.

1819–1827	The Cherokee Nation undertakes a vast assimilation program in an attempt to remain in their homelands.
1821	Sequoyah presents his syllabary to the Cherokee people.
1825	New Echota is established as the capital of the Cherokee Nation.
1827	William Hicks is elected principal chief of the Cherokee Nation at the first national convention.
1828	John Ross is elected principal chief of the Cherokee Nation; first issue of the *Cherokee Phoenix* is published.
1829	Georgia passes its notorious anti-Cherokee laws.
1830	President Andrew Jackson's Indian Removal Bill is passed into law.
1831	The U.S. Supreme Court rules against the Cherokee in *Cherokee Nation v. Georgia*; Reverends Elizur Butler and Samuel Worcester are thrown into prison for refusing to swear to a Georgia loyalty oath.
1832	The Supreme Court rules against Worcester's conviction in *Worcester v. Georgia*.
1835	The Treaty Party meets with U.S. negotiators on December 29 and signs the fraudulent Treaty of New Echota, allowing for removal of the Cherokee.
1836–1838	About 2,000 Cherokee voluntarily remove themselves and join the Western Cherokee in Arkansas.
1838	The forced removal of the Cherokee begins.
1839	The last detachment of Cherokee arrive at Fort Gibson— the Trail of Tears is over; the Cherokee Nation under Chief Ross and the Western Cherokee reunite; Treaty Party members Elias Boudinot, Major Ridge, and John Ridge are killed.
1841–1846	A Cherokee civil war rages.
1846	A treaty signed by the Cherokee Nation, the Western Cherokee, and the Treaty Party brings an end to the violence of the last several years.

1846–1859	The Cherokee Nation is rebuilt; this period is often called the Golden Age of the Cherokee Nation.
1861	Stand Watie raises Cherokee Confederate troops; to keep the Cherokee Nation from becoming divided, Chief John Ross signs a treaty with the Confederacy.
1862	Union troops arrest Ross, who repudiates the Confederate treaty.
1865	General Robert E. Lee surrenders at Appomattox in April; Stand Watie surrenders in June, the last Confederate general to surrender.
1866	Reconstruction treaty is signed at Fort Smith; John Ross dies shortly afterward.
1868	U.S. Congress officially recognizes the Eastern Band as a distinct tribe.
1887	James Mooney begins his field work among the Eastern Cherokee.
1900	Mooney's *Myths of the Cherokee* is published.
1907	Oklahoma becomes a state, combining Oklahoma Territory and Indian Territory.
1936	Congress passes the Oklahoma Indian General Welfare Act.
1941	President Franklin D. Roosevelt appoints Jesse Bartley Milam as principal chief of the Cherokee Nation; he remains chief until his death in 1949.
1946	Under the Oklahoma Indian General Welfare Act, the United Keetoowah Band of Cherokee Indians in Oklahoma is established and approved; Jim Pickup is elected the band's first principal chief.
1949	Jesse Bartley Milam dies; President Harry Truman appoints W.W. Keeler to replace him.
1950	The historical pageant *Unto These Hills* has its debut in Cherokee, North Carolina.
1970	Congress passes a law to give elections back to the Cherokee Nation.

1971	In its first election, the Cherokee Nation elects W.W. Keeler as principal chief.
1975	Ross Swimmer is elected principal chief of the Cherokee Nation.
1984	The councils of the Cherokee Nation and the Eastern Band of Cherokee Indians meet together in a joint council at Red Clay, Tennessee, for the first time in 146 years.
1985	Wilma Mankiller becomes the first woman chief of the Cherokee Nation when Swimmer resigns to become head of the Bureau of Indian Affairs.
1996	The Eastern Band of Cherokee Indians purchases the site of old Keetoowah, said to be the Mother Town of the Cherokees; ceremonies are held there once again.
2007	The Cherokee Nation votes to exclude from tribal membership anyone lacking Cherokee blood, thus disenfranchising descendants of the former black slaves of Cherokees. The freedmen were given Cherokee citizenship in the 1866 Reconstruction treaty.

Glossary

aboriginal The first or original of its kind in a region.

Algonquian A Native American language family.

allotment A piece of land assigned to an individual.

ambiguous Capable of being understood in more than one way.

amnesty A pardon granted by the government to a group of people.

anetsa The ballplay, or Cherokee stick ball.

Ani yunwi ya "The Real People" or "Original People." The Cherokee called themselves by this name. *Ani* is a plural indicator like the "s" on the end of an English word; *yunwi* means a person; and *ya* is an intensive. The word eventually came to mean "Indian."

anthropologist One who studies human beings through time in relation to their culture.

antiquarian One who collects or studies old things.

Bureau of Indian Affairs The government agency that oversees the business of Indian tribes. Originally located in the War Department, it is now in the Department of the Interior.

cession The act of giving something up. In the case of Indian treaties, what was given up was usually land.

Chickasaw A Muskogean Southeastern Indian tribe.

Choctaw A Muskogean Southeastern Indian tribe, originally part of the Chickasaw.

chunkey Creek name for a traditional Cherokee game. See *gatayusti*.

clan A family in which descent is traced solely through one parental line. The Cherokee clans are matrilineal, traced through the female line.

creation cycle A series of stories that explains the way the world was made and how things came to be the way they are.

Creek A Muskogean Southeastern Indian tribe.

culture   The sum of all lifeways of a people, the beliefs and habits, the things that make them who they are.

federally recognized tribes   Indian tribes that have a special relationship with the federal government.

Five Civilized Tribes   Because the Cherokee, Choctaw, Chickasaw, Creek, and Seminole began to dress like whites and otherwise imitate the white man's culture in the 1820s and 1830s, they became known as the Five Civilized Tribes. The term is avoided these days, since it implies that the five tribes were not civilized before that time and that other Indian tribes were not civilized at all.

freedmen   Former slaves of members of the Five Tribes. They were supposed to have been made citizens of the various tribes at the end of the Civil War. The term also refers to their descendants today.

gatayusti   A game played by the Cherokee and other Southeastern Indians, in which a stone disc is thrown and a spear is tossed after it. The object is to have the spear point touch the stone when it stops rolling. Indians used to bet on this game. The Creek call it chunkey, and the game is usually called that today since the word is much easier for non-Cherokee speakers to say.

Iroquoian   A language family and a political league.

Jesuit   A member of the Catholic order founded by St. Ignatius Loyola and dedicated to missionary work and education.

Jisdu   Cherokee for rabbit. It may also be spelled Tsisdu. Jisdu is the Cherokee trickster. See *trickster*.

jurisdiction   The limits in which authority may be exercised.

Keetoowah   It is the name of an old Cherokee town, said to be the mother town of the Cherokee. Kituwah and Giduwa are alternative spellings. The Cherokee sometimes call themselves Ani-Kituwagi or Keetoowah People. The site of old Kituwah is once again owned by Cherokees. Keetoowah is also the name of an ancient Cherokee society, dedicated to preserving the Cherokee language and culture, and it is the name of a Cherokee tribal government, the United Keetoowah Band of Cherokee Indians in Oklahoma.

Lighthorse   Name of the national police forces of the Cherokee, Choctaw, Creek, Chickasaw, and Seminole tribes until the end of the Civil War.

matrilineal   Descent that is traced only through the female line. In a matrilineal clan, the father is almost irrelevant. A child belongs to its mother's clan.

Muskogean   A linguistic family. The Creek, Seminole, Choctaw, and Chickasaw belong to this group.

Occaneechi   A Southeastern Indian tribe.

oral tradition   The tales, songs, and other literary material that any culture preserved by telling and passing them along orally, before they were written down and in many cases before that culture had writing.

principal chief   Originally, the Cherokee had many chiefs, at least two for each town. So when they needed a name for their newly established chief executive, they called him the principal chief, or the main chief of many chiefs.

Red Stick Creek   A faction of the Creek who were at war with the United States in 1813. U.S. troops under Andrew Jackson, assisted by other Creeks and by the Cherokee, eventually defeated the Red Sticks.

Shawnee   A Southeastern Algonquian Indian tribe.

Siouan   A language family. Several Siouan-speaking tribes lived in the old Southeast.

smoke shop   A shop that sells tobacco products. If the shop is owned by an Indian and is on "Indian land" or "trust land," it is not required to collect state tobacco taxes. Therefore the cigarettes and other products are sold at lower prices. Non-Indian tobacco sellers near Indian smoke shops feel that this is unfair.

sovereignty   The highest authority within a specified region. Indian tribes are deemed to have limited sovereignty in their jurisdictions. Their sovereignty is limited because of specific treaties and specific federal laws.

syllabary   A writing system in which the symbols (letters) represent the sounds of syllables.

Termination   A government program of the 1950s in which the government ended its relationship with certain Indian tribes.

treaty   An agreement between two sovereign nations.

trickster   A character in many Indian tales from the oral traditions. He is almost always an animal. In the Southeast he is a rabbit. On the plains he is mostly a coyote. He represents humankind, sometimes mean and stingy, other times heroic.

Tsalagi The Cherokee pronunciation of "Cherokee." It is sometimes spelled Chalagi, sometimes Jalagi. It probably came from the Choctaw jargon that was widely used in the Southeast and was based on the Choctaw language. The Choctaw word for Cherokee is Chalakee.

Tuscarora A southeastern Indian tribe.

Weesock A southeastern Indian tribe.

Yamasee A southeastern Indian tribe.

Bibliography

Anderson, William L., ed. *Cherokee Removal: Before and After*. Athens: University of Georgia Press, 1989.

——. *A Cherokee Encyclopedia*. Albuquerque: University of New Mexico Press, 2007.

Conley, Robert J. *The Cherokee Nation: A History*. Albuquerque: University of New Mexico Press, 1999.

——. *Cherokee Americans: The Eastern Band of Cherokees in the Twentieth Century*. Lincoln: University of Nebraska Press, 1991.

Finger, John R. *The Eastern Band of Cherokees 1819–1900*. Knoxville: University of Tennessee Press, 1984.

——. *The Five Civilized Tribes*. Norman: University of Oklahoma Press, 1953.

Foreman, Grant. *Indian Removal: The Emigration of the Five Civilized Tribes of Indians*. Norman: University of Oklahoma, 1986.

——. *Sequoyah*. Norman: University of Oklahoma Press, 1938.

Leeds, Georgia Rae. *The United Keetoowah Band of Cherokee Indians in Oklahoma*. New York: Peter Lang Publishing, 1996.

Meredith, Howard L. *Bartley Milam: Principal Chief of the Cherokee Nation*. Muskogee, Okla.: Indian University Press, Bacone College, 1985.

Mooney, James. *Myths of the Cherokee and Sacred Formulas of the Cherokee*. Bureau of American Ethnology, 19th and 7th Annual Reports, reproduced 1982 by Charles and Randy Elder, Booksellers.

Moulton, Gary. *John Ross: Cherokee Chief*. Athens: University of Georgia Press, 1978.

Perdue, Theda and Michael Green. *The Cherokee Removal: A Brief History with Documents*. New York: Bedford/St. Martins, 2004.

Perdue, Theda. *Cherokee Women: Gender and Culture Change 1700-1835*. Lincoln, Neb: Bison Books, 1999.

Royce, Charles C. *The Cherokee Nation of Indians*. Chicago: Aldine Publishing, 1975.

Southeast Tennessee Cherokee Native American Guide, an undated pamphlet, focusing mainly on the Trail of Tears, published by Southeast Tennessee Tourism Association.

Van Every, Dale. *Disinherited: The Lost Birthright of the American Indian*. New York: William Morrow, 1966.

Wardell, Morris L. *A Political History of the Cherokee Nation, 1838–1907*. Norman: University of Oklahoma Press, 1977.

Washburn, Cephas. *Reminiscences of the Indians*. Presbyterian Committee of Publication, Richmond, n.d., Johnson Reprint Corporation, New York, 1971.

Wilkins, Thurman. *Cherokee Tragedy: The Ridge Family and the Decimation of a People*. Norman: University of Oklahoma Press, 1986.

Woodward, Grace Steele. *The Cherokees*. Norman: University of Oklahoma Press, 1963

Further Resources

Collier, Peter. *When Shall They Rest? The Cherokees' Long Struggle with America*. New York: Holt, Rinehart, and Winston, 1973.

———. *Cherokee Dragon*. Norman: University of Oklahoma Press, 2001.

———. *Cherokee Thoughts: Honest and Uncensored*. Norman: University of Oklahoma Press, 2008.

———. *The Dark Island* (Real People series), New York: Doubleday, 1995.

———. *The Dark Way* (Real People series). New York: Doubleday, 1993.

———. *The Long Way Home* (Real People series), New York: Doubleday, 1994.

———. *Mountain Windsong: A Novel of the Trail of Tears.* Norman: University of Oklahoma Press, 1992.

———. *The Peace Chief.* Norman: Red River Books/University of Oklahoma Press, 2001.

———. *Sequoyah.* New York: St. Martin's Press, 2002.

———. *Spanish Jack*. New York: St. Martin's Press, 2001.

———. *War Trail North* (Real People series), New York: Doubleday, 1995.

———. *War Woman*. Norman: Red River Books/University of Oklahoma Press, 2001.

Conley, Robert J. *The Way of the Priests* (Real People series). New York: Doubleday, 1992.

———. *The Way South* (Real People series), New York: Doubleday, 1994.

———. *The White Path* (Real People series). New York: Doubleday, 1993.

Duncan, Barbara, ed. *Living Stories of the Cherokee*. Chapel Hill: University of North Carolina Press, 1998.

Ehle, John. *Trail of Tears: The Rise and Fall of the Cherokee Nation*. New York: Anchor Books, 1988.

Gaines, W. Craig. *The Confederate Cherokees: John Drew's Regiment of Mounted Rifles*. Baton Rouge: Louisiana State University Press, 1989.

Hudson, Charles. *The Southeastern Indians*. Knoxville: University of Tennessee Press, 1976.

Starr, Emmet. *History of the Cherokee Indians*, reprint. Oklahoma City: The Warden Company, 1921.

Strickland, Rennard. *Fire and the Spirits: Cherokee Law from Clan to Court.* Norman: University of Oklahoma Press, 1975.

Thornton, Russell. *The Cherokees: A Population History.* Lincoln: University of Nebraska Press, 1990.

Web Sites

Cherokee Heritage Center

http://www.cherokeeheritage.org

Cherokee Nation

http://www.cherokee.org

The Eastern Band of Cherokee Indians

http://nc-cherokee.com

Museum of the Cherokee Indian

http://www.cherokeemuseum.org

Native Languages of the Americas: Cherokee

http://www.native-languages.org/cherokee.htm

United Keetoowah Band of Cherokee Indians

http://www.keetoowahcherokee.org

Picture Credits

PAGE:

15:   Adam Jones/Visuals Unlimited, Inc/Getty Images

22:   © Underwood & Underwood/CORBIS

27:   The Granger Collection, NYC — All rights reserved.

31:   The Granger Collection, NYC — All rights reserved.

41:   © Infobase Learning

43:   The Granger Collection, NYC — All rights reserved.

48:   Private Collection / Peter Newark American Pictures / The Bridgeman Art Library

51:   The Granger Collection, NYC — All rights reserved.

54:   The Granger Collection, NYC — All rights reserved.

56:   © Infobase Learning

60:   © Infobase Learning

63:   Apic/Hulton Archive/ Getty Images

65:   Private Collection / Peter Newark Western Americana / The Bridgeman Art Library

69:   Dennis Cook/AP Images

76:   Rue des Archives / The Granger Collection, NYC — All rights reserved.

81:   © David Lyons / Alamy

87:   A. Cuervo/Tulsa World/AP Images

Index

A

Ada gal'kala (Attakullakulla), 30
  John Stuart and, 34
  son of, 36
  "treaty" of Sycamore Shoals and, 35
Adams, Bud, 87
Adams, John, 40
Alabama, 14, 26, 40
allotments, 66, 77. *See also* Dawes Act;
  General Allotment Act
alphabet, creation of, 43
ancestral homeland, reduction of, 41
anetsa game, 23
anti-Cherokee laws
  bills passed, 45
  injunction against, 47
  lawsuit against, 46–49
Appalachian Mountains, 14
Appomatox, Virginia, 61
Arkansas, 26, 40, 47, 84
Arthur, Gabriel, 27–29
Articles of Agreement, 30
Ayunini. *See* Swimmer, Ross

B

balance, harmony and, 24
ballplay, 23–24, 75, 78
basket makers, 77
Battle of Horseshoe Bend, 42
Battle of Mabila, 27
Beck, Polly, 63–64
Beck's Mill, 62–64
Bell, John, 53
Benge, Bob, 37
bingo operations, 80, 83, 85
birthplace of tribe, 15
Black Jack Davy (Oskison), 18
Blackfox, 40
Blanket, 40
Bloody Fellow, 37
Boone, Daniel, 35
Boudinot, Elias
  newspaper work of, 44, 49
  novel by, 18
  treaty signing by, 49, 57
Bowl/Bowles (chief), 38
"Br'er Rabbit and the Tar-Baby" (tale),
  17
Brothers Three (Oskison), 18
Bureau of Indian Affairs, 76, 83, 84, 85
Bushyhead, George, 75
Butler, Elizur, 49, 50

C

casinos, 73, 80, 85, 89
census, 67, 74
ceremonies, 24
Charlestown (Charleston), South Caro-
  lina, 29
Cherokee, North Carolina, 14, 79
Cherokee Advocate, 59, 62
Cherokee Agency, 53
Cherokee Americans, 77
Cherokee Fair, 77
"Cherokee" groups, 86
"Cherokee Kid, The," 19
Cherokee Mountains, 14
Cherokee Nation
  "chiefs for a day," 68
  college graduates from, 67
  council of, 62
  Creek War and, 39
  dismantling of, 66–67
  first female chief of, 69
  Golden Age of, 59
  government reorganization, 45
  headquarters of, 86
  Keetoowah Band and, 84
  legal matters and, 46–49, 82
  membership/citizenship, 72, 86
  missionaries in, 49
  politics and, 68–73
  school system of, 59
  Trail of Tears, aftermath of, 57–58
  Western Cherokee and, 57
Cherokee Nation: A History, The, 36
Cherokee Nation, The, 52
Cherokee Nation v. Georgia, 47, 49

Cherokee National Holiday, 85
Cherokee Night, The (Riggs), 18
Cherokee Phoenix, 49
Cherokee Proud (McClure), 86
Chickamauga Creek, 37
Chickamaugans, 37, 38, 40
Chickasaw Nation, 61
Chicken, George, 30
Choctaw Nation, 61
Chota, Tennessee, 28, 29
Christians/Christianity, 39, 74
chunkey game, 23
citizenship
    of Cherokee Nation, 72, 86
    Indian Citizenship Act of 1924, 78
    tribal, 72
    voter's rights and, 79
Civil War
    Confederacy and, 61, 63
    Indian Territory during, 60
    last shot fired in, 61
    outbreak of, 75
    period following, 62
    Unionist, 75
"civilization," 45
clans, 21–22
Clemson, South Carolina, 30
Climber, the, 17
Clinton, Bill, 69
Collier, John, 79
colonial wars, 33–37
    England and, 35
    Highlanders/Royal Scots and, 33
    Oconostota and, 34
    "treaty" of Sycamore Shoals, 35–37
Confederacy, 61, 63
Conley, Robert J., 18
Conley's Sharpshooters, 61
craftspeople, 77, 79, 82, 88
creation stories, 16–18
Creek Nation, 61
Creek War, 39
culture, 88–89
Cuming, Alexander, 30, 31
Curtis Act, 66
customs, 75

D

Daltons, the, 62
dances, 23, 75, 88
Dawes Act, 65–66
Dawes Commission, 66
de Soto, Hernando, 26, 27
Deas, Edward, 53

Degadoga, 40
Descendants of Freedmen of the Five
    Civilized Tribes, 73
disease, 32
Doublehead, 37
Downing, Lewis, 62, 64
Dragging Canoe (Tsiyu Gansini), 35–37
Drane, Gus, 53
Drew, John, 42
Drowning Bear (chief), 73
Dugan, Joyce (chief), 20
Duke Energy, 85
Dwight Mission, 40, 47

E

Eastern Band, 61, 73–80
    casinos and, 89
    federal assistance and, 80
    land issues and, 75–76
    population of, 87
    tourism and, 81
    voter's rights and, 78
Eastern Band of Cherokees: 1819–1900
    (Finger), 75
Eastern Cherokee, 76–77
Edohi, Ama, 30
education
    college graduates, 67
    language and, 80, 85
    school system, 59
"Emperor of the Cherokees," 30
England
    allegiance to, 31
    Cherokee to, 35
    Indian land and, 35
    trading with, 30
    at war in Europe, 33
Englishmen, 27–29
Euchella, 73

F

federal court, 62
federal government, 82. *See also* government
    ambiguous policies of, 82
    funding by, 85, 89
    "Great Society" social reforms, 80
    land holdings and, 65, 66, 76
federally recognized tribes, 84, 86
federal-tribal relationship, 79
Finger, John R., 75, 77
Five Civilized Tribes, 61, 73
Flying Squirrel (chief), 75
folk story. *See* oral tradition

Foreman, James, 57
Fort Loudoun, Tennessee, 34
Fort Payne, Alabama, 53
Fort Sill, Oklahoma, 64
Fort Smith, Arkansas, 62, 64
France/French, the, 30–32, 33
"freedmen," 72–73

G

games, 23–24
gaming establishments, 73
   bingo operations, 80, 83, 85
   casinos, 80, 85, 89
gatayusti game, 23
General Allotment Act, 65. *See also* al-
   lotments
George II (king), 30
Georgia, 14, 26, 42
   anti-Cherokee laws in, 45
   removal from, 51
Georgia Compact, 40
Georgia Guard, 49
Gist, Nathaniel, 46
Glancy, Diane, 18
Glory, Bill, 82–83
Going Snake, 42
Golden Age, 59
Gordon, Jim (chief), 83
government, 20–21. *See also* federal
   government
   dismantling of, 65, 66–67
   "petticoat government," 25
Grant, Ulysses S., 61
Gray, Wanda, 84
Great Smoky Mountains National Park,
   79
"Great Society" social reforms, 80
Great Spirit, 39
green corn dance, 75, 78
Green Grow the Lilacs (Riggs), 18
Gulager, Clu, 87

H

Hair, John (chief), 83
harmony, balance and, 24
Harrah's Cherokee Casino, 80
Harris, Joel Chandler, 17
Hart, Nathaniel, 35, 36
Henderson, Richard, 35, 36
Hicks, Michell (chief), 80
Hicks, William, 45
Hobson, Geary, 18
housing authority, 83

I

identity, 88
Indian Citizenship Act of 1924, 78
"Indian Cowboy," 19
Indian Removal Act, 46. *See also* Re-
   moval, the
Indian Self-Determination and Educa-
   tion Assistance Act, 80
Indian Territory
   during Civil War, 60
   creation of, 61, 62
   Curtis Act and, 66
   Dawes Act and, 66
   jurisdictional confusion in, 62–64
   land routes to, 53
   lawlessness in, 62
   Oklahoma Territory and, 67
Iroquoian tribes, 14
Iroquois Confederacy, 29

J

Jackson, Andrew, 42, 45, 46, 51
James, Jesse, 62
Jefferson, Thomas, 40
Jidsu (Rabbit) trickster, 17
Johnson, Lyndon, 80
Junaluska, 42
Justice, Dick, 40

K

Keeler, Bill (chief), 82
Keetoowah Band. *See* United Keetoowah
   Band
Kentucky, 14, 35
Kesterton, Mr., 62–64
Kituwah mound, 20

L

land holdings
   allotments, 66, 77
   ancient homeland, 44
   Andrew Jackson and, 42
   Dawes Act and, 65–66
   Eastern Band and, 75–76
   king of England and, 35
   land run for, 65
   reduction in, 39, 41
language, 88. *See also* syllabary
   dialects, 20
   literacy and, 43, 74
   programs, 80, 85
   written, 43, 47
Lee, Robert E., 61

Leeds, Georgia Rae, 82
*Life and Adventures of Joaquin Murieta,
   The* (Ridge), 18
literacy rates, 74
Little Tennessee, 28
Lower Towns, 20, 34
Lowrey, John, 39, 42
Luftee, the, 73

M

Madison, James, 39, 48
Mankiller, Wilma (chief), 69, 83, 84
Marshall, John, 47, 49
matrilineal society, 22
McAlister, Barbara, 87
McClure, Tony Mack, 86
Meigs, R.J., 57
Memoirs (Timberlake), 34
Mexico, 47, 86
Middle Towns, 20
missionaries, 47, 49
Mississippi, 26
Mississippi River, 42, 46, 55, 57
Missouri, 40
Montgomery, Archibald, 33
Mooney, James, 14, 16, 77
Mother Town, 20
Museum of the Cherokee Indian, 79, 81
Myths of the Cherokee (Mooney), 20, 77

N

Nanyehi, 25
Napoleon, 37
National Council, 39, 45, 47
nationalists, 62
"Nations," 62
Native Americans, 78, 79, 84. *See also
   specific tribe*
Needham, James, 27–28
New Echota, Georgia, 45
   Treaty of New Echota, 49, 50, 57, 73
New Madrid, Missouri, 40
Nicolson, Francis, 29
North Carolina, 14, 84
   Cherokee origins in, 15
   Eastern Band in, 61, 86
   Qualla Boundary in, 52
   voter's rights in, 78

O

Occaneechi Indians, 28
Oconaluftee, the, 73
Oconaluftee Indian Village, 79, 81

Oconaluftee River, 73
Oconostota (war chief)
   Christian Priber and, 32
   colonial wars and, 34
   "treaty" of Sycamore Shoals and, 35
"Ode to Sequoyah" (poem), 44–45
Ohio, 40
Oklahoma, 51, 65–67
   allotment and, 77
   Cherokee Tribe of, 82
   De Soto expedition and, 26
   industries, locating, 82
   statehood of, 67
Oklahoma (play), 18
Oklahoma Territory
   Indian Territory and, 67
   land run in, 65
   organization of, 65
Old Settlers, 40
"Only the Master Shall Praise" (short
   story), 18
opposites/opposing forces, 24
oral tradition
   best-known story, 14–16
   creation stories, 16–18
   Western Cherokee and, 40, 42
orphanage, 59
Orr, James, 37
Osage, 50
Oskison, John Milton, 18
Ostenaco, 35
Out of Dust (Riggs), 18
outlaws, 62

P

Parker, Isaac, 62
Pearis, Richard, 36
Pickup, Jim, 82
Pierce, Earl Boyd, 82
Plains Indians, 79
Poor Sarah, or The Indian Woman
   (Boudinot), 18
population numbers, tribes, 87
Posey, Alex, 44
Post, Wiley, 19
Presidential Medal of Freedom, 69
Priber, Christian Gottlieb, 31–32, 40
Proctor, Johnson, 64
Proctor, Zeke, 62–64
pro-treaty Cherokee, 51, 53

Q

Qualla Boundary, 52, 74, 76, 79, 86

Qualla Cherokee, 73, 74
Quallatown, 73, 74

R

Rabbit (Jidsu) trickster, 17
race
    Dawes Commission roll and, 72
    family names and, 35, 66
    full-blood, 36, 62, 67
    mixed blood, 35, 66, 67, 88
Reconstruction era, 62
Red Stick Creeks, 46
Reformed Keetoowahs, 84
religious rituals, 24
Reminiscences of the Indians, 42
Removal, the, 73–74, 78. *See also* Indian
    Removal Act
    deadline for, 51
    routes of removal, 56
Removal Treaty, 49, 52
reservation(s)
    Cherokee Fair at, 77
    Eastern Band and, 73
    gaming establishments, 80
    Qualla Boundary, 52, 79, 86
Revolutionary War, 37
Ridge, John Rollin, 18, 49, 50
Ridge, Major, 42, 49, 50
Riggs, Rollie Lynn, 18
Rogers, Will, 18, 19, 22, 67
Rogers, William C. (chief), 67
Roosevelt, Franklin, 79
Ross, John (chief), 42, 49, 53, 57–58
    Civil War and, 61
    death of, 62
    of Keetoowah, 84
    as principal chief, 45
    Trail of Tears and, 50, 51, 54, 55
Ross Papers, 39
Ross Party, 57
Ross's Landing, 53

S

sacred flame, 20
Saunook, Stilwell, 77
school system, 59
Selective Service Act of 1917, 77
"seminaries," 59
Seminole Nation, 61
Sequoyah, 42
    alphabet creation by, 43
    Cherokee Nation and, 57
    Cherokee syllabary and, 46–47

Sequoyah Training School, 82
Shawnees, the, 33
Singing Bird, The (Oskison), 18
sky vault, 15, 16, 24
slave owners, 61
smallpox epidemic, 32
Smith, Chad (chief), 73, 87, 88–89
Smith, Nimrod Jared (chief), 76, 77
smoke shops, 83–84
Soco Creek, 73
Song of the South (film), 17
South Carolina, 14, 28, 29–30, 31, 34
Southeast, 14, 29
sovereignty, tribal, 72, 73, 85
Spaniards, 26–27, 28
Sperry, Oklahoma, 83
spirituality, 24
Starr, James, 57
Starr family, 57
stickball, 23–24
stomp dances, 23, 88
stories. *See* oral tradition
Stuart, Henry, 36
Stuart, John "Bushyhead," 34
Studi, Wes, 87
surnames, 35
Swimmer, Ross (chief)
    Bureau of Indian Affairs and, 83
    culture, traditions and, 76
    death of, 77
    election of, 70
    James Mooney and, 77, 78
Sycamore Shoals, "treaty" of, 35–37
syllabary, 46–47

T

Tahlequah, Oklahoma, 59, 62, 83, 86
Ta-ka-e-tuh, 42
Taskagi, 46
Tellico Blockhouse, 37
Tennessee, 14, 26, 35, 42, 84
Tennessee Titans football team, 87
Termination policy, 80, 81–82
Texas Jack's Wild West Circus, 19
"The Problem of Old Harjo" (short
    story), 18
Thomas, William
    Civil War and, 61
    raised by the Cherokee, 52
Thomas, William Holland, 73
    Cherokee Company and, 74
    death of, 77
    as legislator, 75
Thomas Gilcrease Institute of American

History and Art, 39
Thomas Legion, 61
timber industry, 77, 79
Timberlake, Henry, 34, 35
tourism, 79, 80
traditionalist, 77, 80
Trail of Tears, 50–58
    aftermath of, 57–58
    Chief John Ross and, 50, 51, 54, 55, 57
    deadline for removal, 51
    routes of removal, 56
    stockades and, 52–53
    written account of, 53
Transylvania Land Company, 35
treaty
    with the Confederacy, 61
    of 1819, 73
    of 1866, 62, 63, 73
    of New Echota, 49, 50, 57, 73
    Removal Treaty, 49, 52
    with South Carolina/Virginia, 34
    "treaty" of Sycamore Shoals, 35–37
Treaty Party, 57, 58
tribal sovereignty, 72, 73
tribes, federally recognized, 86
Tsalagi, 18, 20
Tsali, 52, 73–74
Tuscarora, the, 29
Tuskaloosa (chief), 27

U

Uncle Remus tales, 17
United Keetoowah Band of Cherokee Indians in Oklahoma, The (Leeds), 82
United Keetoowah Band (UKB), 80–85
    Cherokee Nation and, 84
    gaming establishments, 85, 89
    headquarters of, 86
    Keetoowah, sacred site, 85
    Keetoowah Society, 80
    population of, 87
Unto These Hills (play), 79
Upper Towns, 20
U.S. Supreme Court, 47
Usdi, Wil (Little Will), 73

V

Vian, Oklahoma, 83–84
Vinyard Post Office, Arkansas, 53
Virginia, 14, 33
    colony of, 28
    peace treaties with, 34
voter's rights, 79

W

Waldron, Arkansas, 84
Walker, John, 50
War Woman, 25
Ward, Nancy, 36–37
Washburn, Cephas, 40, 42
Washington, D.C., 58
Waterloo, Alabama, 53
Watie, Stand
    camp in Arkansas, 58
    Civil War and, 61, 63
    in poem, 44
    trial of, 57
Watts, John, 37
Waynesville, North Carolina, 61
Weesock Indians, 28
West Virginia, 14
Western Carolina University, 80
Western Cherokee Nation, 50, 57, 58
    Dwight Mission and, 40
    land ceded and, 42
    new treaty and, 58
    Old Settlers name, 40
    stories/oral tradition, 40, 42
    syllabary and, 47
    Treaty of New Echota and, 50, 57
White Path, 42
white society, 25, 28
    Cuming and Priber, 30–32
    Englishmen, 27–29
    farmers, 20
    incursion of, 25, 40
    Spaniards, 26–27
Whiteley, R.H.K., 53
Wickliffe, George (chief), 85
Wild Harvest (Oskison), 18
Wirt, William, 46, 49
women
    matrilineal society and, 22
    power of, 24–25
Wood, Abraham, 29
Wool, John Ellis, 52
Worcester, Samuel, 49, 50, 59
Worcester v. Georgia, 49
World War I, 77
World War II, 79
Wrosetasatow, 30
Wuh-teh, 46

Y

Yamasee, the, 29
Yellow Hill, 76
Yonaguska (Drowning Bear), 73, 74

About the Contributors

Robert J. Conley, a tribal member of the Cherokee Nation, has written more than 80 books, including *The Cherokee Nation: A History*. Conley has taught at several colleges and universities and received his master's degree in English from Midwestern University in 1968.

Series editor **Paul C. Rosier** received his Ph.D. in American History from the University of Rochester in 1998. Dr. Rosier currently serves as Associate Professor of History at Villanova University (Villanova, Pennsylvania), where he teaches Native American History, American Environmental History, Global Environmental Justice Movements, History of American Capitalism, and World History.

In 2001, the University of Nebraska Press published his first book, *Rebirth of the Blackfeet Nation, 1912–1954*; in 2003, Greenwood Press published *Native American Issues* as part of its Contemporary Ethnic American Issues series. In 2006, he coedited an international volume called *Echoes from the Poisoned Well: Global Memories of Environmental Injustice*. Dr. Rosier has also published articles in the *American Indian Culture and Research Journal*, the *Journal of American Ethnic History*, and the *Journal of American History*. His *Journal of American History* article, entitled "They Are Ancestral Homelands: Race, Place, and Politics in Cold War Native America, 1945–1961," was selected for inclusion in *The Ten Best History Essays of 2006–2007*, published by Palgrave MacMillan in 2008; and it won the Western History Association's 2007 Arrell Gibson Award for Best Essay on the history of Native Americans. His latest book, *Serving Their Country: American Indian Politics and Patriotism in the Twentieth Century* (Harvard University Press), is winner of the 2010 Labriola Center American Indian National Book Award.